Managing Your Boss

Christie Kennard

W0006366

Gower

First published in the USA by National Press
Publications, Inc. as *How to Manage Your Boss*
This edition published by
Gower Publishing Limited
Gower House
Croft Road
Aldershot
Hampshire GU11 3HR
England

British Library Cataloguing in Publication Data
Kennard, Christie
    Managing your boss
    1. Industrial relations   2. Communication in
    industrial relations   3. Interpersonal relations
    I. Title
    658. 3'145

ISBN 0 566 07830 9

Printed in Great Britain by Biddles Ltd, Guildford

Contents

vi   *Contents*

1

Why is managing a boss so important?

Just when you thought you had enough responsibilities at work, someone introduces the concept of managing your boss. 'I've got enough to do without having to manage my boss,' you say. 'After all, it's my boss's job to manage me. Right?' Wrong.

By learning how to manage your boss, you'll not only make both your jobs easier, you'll build a personal power base that can help you get where you want to go. No matter what your position in a company (unless you own it 100 per cent), you will always have a boss. A key to making this relationship work better for you both is that management is a two-way street. Subordinates must take more responsibility for the flow of information and feed-back. It's a growing fact of corporate life that the burden for managing the relationship should no longer fall entirely on the boss.

It's easy for subordinates to feel otherwise. If your boss is weak, unfocused or incompetent, you may want to avoid the relationship as much as possible. Similarly, when you're working for a boss who keeps dumping work on you, is adversarial in atti-tude or too authoritative, it's easy to respond with passivity.

Yet such attitudes are not only counter-produc-tive, they defeat the professional image you want to project to others in your company.

What does managing your boss mean?

It means consciously working with your boss to obtain the best possible results for the two of you and your company.

The first step in mastering this process begins by learning how to manage yourself and take com-mand of the situation, no matter what your place on the corporate ladder.

Learning how to become a strong leader shows your boss two things: that you know how to take charge of yourself and that you are a depend-able and trustworthy ally. Being dependable and honest with your boss creates an important pro-fessional relationship that can be a rock-solid foundation to your career and your future with the company.

Managing your boss also means you have the ability to work within the structure and gain resources, support and fair treatment. And should you have to work with others outside the chain of command, your boss's support and influence can be invaluable.

Be aware of the four basic steps required to build a good relationship with your boss:

1. Make an honest self-appraisal of your own needs, objectives and working style.

2. Get as much detailed information as possible about your boss's goals, strengths, skills, weaknesses, preferred working style and pressures he or she is working under.

3. Create a relationship that fits both of your key needs and styles.

4. Take time to maintain the relationship. Keep your boss informed of your feelings and expectations, especially as they change.

In the following pages, these four basic steps will be examined in detail and you'll learn to identify different management styles. Your relationship with your boss can have far-reaching consequences that affect not only your future, but your company's future as well.

In a later chapter, 'Bad bosses, what they can do to you, how you can stop them', specific scenarios will give you ways to work through a relationship with a boss who might have seemed impossible until now.

Managing your boss will give you an increased awareness of your role and your boss's role – how they're the same and how they differ. And, who knows, you might even find out that your boss is not such a bad person after all.

2

Understanding how to use power

Once upon a time in the 1970s, organizations began experimenting with a new power structure – the flattened pyramid.

If you're asking yourself, 'What's this got to do with me?' the answer is 'Everything'! Understanding the hierarchical nature of the corporate pyramid, its pathways of power and how they've changed, is crucial to how you'll manage your boss. In this chapter we'll examine:

- why power pyramids exist and how they work;

- what kind of power your boss has;
- what kind of power you have.

The power pyramid

Whether your company has one boss and one employee or one managing director and 800 employees, there's a power pyramid at work: the big boss is at the capstone giving orders and the employees are at the base executing them.

The pyramid as a model for modern corporate structure originates in military history – Caesar's legions and Napoleon's Imperial Army. During the Second World War, it became the ideal way to pattern work relationships. The managing director at the top fulfilled the same role as a five-star general, and the workers at the bottom were similar to army recruits.

By tracing the job titles downward in the following list you can see how authority is delegated from one unit of authority to its logical subordinate in the corporate pyramid. Identify your job title or rank, and place yourself somewhere on this list.

Chairman

Chief Executive

Managing Director

Deputy Managing Director

Departmental Director

Other Director

Senior Manager

Middle Manager

First Line Manager

Team Leader/Supervisor

Employee/Worker

Rank and chain of command

The pyramid works because of two concepts: rank, and the chain of command. The lower you are in the pyramid, the less powerful your level or rank.

Except for the managing director at the top and the workers at the bottom, everyone in the corporate pyramid performs the dual tasks of employee and boss. They carry out orders from their immediate boss and issue orders to the strata of employees just beneath them. This is called chain of command and it's the lifeline that filters key information to all parts of the pyramid. It's also a vital concept underlying most interactions in today's corporate world.

The chain of command works because every employee reports to just one boss. The purpose of the pyramid is to divide both large and small tasks into manageable units that are overseen by the bosses and assembled by the employees.

Where's the power?

Typically, the higher your rank, the more power you have. Senior managers and directors have the great-est access to a company's resources and the most responsibility for increasing those resources.

If you're an assistant to someone in upper-level management, count yourself lucky. You're auto-matically positioned closer to the playing field where all the action takes place. But even if you're an employee of a boss further down the pyramid, you still have a chance of getting in the game and wielding some power. How? Simple. By managing your boss.

Why making your boss look good makes you look good

Aside from the substantial rewards you reap from developing a solid working relationship with your boss, managing him carries a more subtle payoff.

Most companies have two sets of rules: explicit and implicit. The *explicit* rules are the ones that are explained during the job interview or the first week on the job. They can be important: your duties, your responsibilities; or they may be trivial: when it's your turn to make coffee, where you may park.

One implicit rule is to be *proactive* rather than *re-active* in your relationship with your boss: to size up the situation at hand and quickly take responsibility.

What are the characteristics of a proactive employee?

- Doesn't wait for the boss to make every move.

- Seeks information and the help needed to do the job.

- Gives the boss feedback, asks questions.

- Initiates action without having to be supervised.

How an employee handles a boss is quite revealing, especially in the first few months of a job. Management keeps its eye on employees who show an ability to define and fulfil their own and their boss's mutual expectations in their working relationship. As opposed to those who only grumble about their bosses, management tags proactive employees as people who are 'going somewhere'.

Clearly, by learning to manage your boss well – even though his position may lack power – you can attract the attention of bigger bosses and perhaps pave the way for a lateral move into the action-packed arena.

What kind of power your boss has

Business analysts have identified several distinct kinds of power, but basically 'boss power' can be broken down into two types: the power of the position and personal power. No matter where your boss's place on the corporate pyramid, it's likely that he wields at least one kind of power. Check which ones fit your boss.

The power of the position

1. *The power to reward*: giving promotions, rises or recognition for a job well done.

2. *The power to punish:* firing or transferring an employee, putting someone in charge of dead-end projects.

3. *Authority:* can be specifically granted, like the right to sign, or can come with the position.

Personal power

1. *Expertise:* being an expert, knowing a function better than anyone else in the company.

2. *Referent power:* charm, charisma, integrity which makes others want to be like them.

3. *Association:* who one knows, being in the right clubs and social groups, marrying the right people.

The first three kinds of power come with the territory. The second three could belong to anyone at any level in the organization – a computer wizard who can handle a crashing system and get it back on line, or a charming middle manager who gives speeches for local volunteer organizations.

It's rare when someone possesses all six kinds of power. Bosses are human, too – strong in some areas, weak in others. Often a boss who is effective and powerful in one arena does not even choose to compete in another. Probably everyone has had the experience of working for the boss's son or daughter who possesses plenty of associative power but is lacking in technical expertise. What about the highly demanding boss who threatens, challenges or competes with employees and makes no claim to personal charm? Review the power list above and ask yourself the following questions:

1. What kind of power does my boss possess?

2. Could he/she use it more effectively?

3. Can I convey that to him/her?

4. What kind of power does my boss need?

5. Can I help him/her get it?

It's best to keep in mind that, according to some management experts, the only real power worth having is the power of position or rank. In most corporate structures, employees quickly learn that no matter how incompetent, lazy or disorganized their boss may be, they are entitled to deference, respect and obedience because of rank – and rank only. It's another one of those implicit corporate rules that complaining about your boss to their boss can constitute corporate suicide. The more hierarchical the structure of your company, the more you're expected to work with your immediate boss, to carry out their orders and be a team player. Absolute deference to your boss is the number one rule.

Even if you're stuck with an incompetent boss in a highly structured company, don't despair! It may come as a surprise to you that, as an employee, you still can wield a great deal of power.

What kind of power you have

Employees have the ability to make their bosses look like kings or fools. They can withhold vital information, give their bosses poor feedback or break the chain of command and route projects through other bosses.

In traditional hierarchical corporations, employees carry out the orders their bosses give them. The bosses have the power and the authority – almost. Employees, however, can undermine their bosses' authority through non-verbal means: by not paying attention when the boss is talking, by not meeting deadlines for reports, by engaging in idle conversation when they need to be working, by 'forgetting' to pass on vital information, or by not sharing expertise. In such ways, subordinates demonstrate to peers and even other bosses that their boss has no real power over them.

Eventually, however, these tactics are unsuccessful and will finally catch up with their perpetrators. They demonstrate behaviour which is unprofessional and demeaning to both you and your boss.

There are better ways you can 'manage upward' and exercise your power in a positive manner. Let's look at some of the same types of boss power we discussed earlier and apply them to you. Identify which kinds of power you use in dealing with your boss.

The power of the position

1. *The power to reward:* making your boss look good, getting him/her out of a jam, giving him/her good feedback.

2. *The power to punish:* programming your boss for failure, withholding information.

3. *Authority:* belonging to organizations with negotiating power like trade unions, political coalitions.

Personal power

1. *Expertise:* being a staff-level expert with a high degree of knowledge in a specialized area, knowing a function better than anyone else in the company.

2. *Referent power:* charm, charisma, integrity that endears individuals to others; easy to talk to; makes others want to be like you.

3. *Association:* who one knows, being in the right social groups, going to the right schools, marrying the right people.

Employees with a certain amount of personal power must be careful not to abuse it. An employee with an MBA from a better school than their boss, or married to the managing director's daughter, could make a middle management boss either resentful or anxious to transfer the employee into another department.

Never underestimate your power – no matter how insignificant your position. Using the power you have to help your boss and the organization shows your boss you understand the value of teamwork. Review the power list above and ask yourself the following questions.

1. What kind of power do I possess?

2. Could I use it more effectively?

3. What kind of power do I need that I don't have?

4. Can I ask my boss to help me get it?

The key to using your power as an employee is to do the best job you can in your present position.

Employees who make no secret of their boredom with their middle management boss, believing their destiny lies in the boardroom, will be left in the dust by more dedicated peers whose bosses have found them reliable and eager.

Summary

1. The power pyramid is the basis of corporate structure. It is built on the dual concepts of rank and chain of command:

   - your boss's position carries certain powers;

   - your position carries certain powers;

   - your relationship with your boss is strengthened when you're proactive rather than reactive.

2. Your boss can wield two kinds of power:

   - The power of the position:

     - power to reward;

     - power to punish;

     - authority inherent in the position.

- Personal power:
  - expertise;
  - referent power;
  - power of association.

3. You, too, can wield similar types of power – either positively or negatively – to make your boss look good or bad.

4. Learn to play your position well. Being willing to work with your boss is the number one rule. Power comes in managing the relationship.

3

Assessing yourself

Before tackling the question of how to manage your boss, it's best to start closer to home and look at how you manage yourself.

You may already be knee-deep in handling the responsibilities of your job with little time, energy or motivation left over at the end of the day. Perhaps you're caught between an unsympathetic boss and uncooperative employees, or perhaps your situation at work couldn't be better. In either case, it's important to make a clear assessment of yourself, your skills and your emotional make-up. For those of you who already manage others or report to managers, it's also necessary to have a clear idea of what management is all about.

In this chapter we'll examine the following concepts:

1. the art of management;

2. managing yourself;

3. assessing yourself.

The art of management

Management is based on describing objectives and measuring performance by bottom-line evaluations of profit and loss.

Managing by objectives means working for measurable results which can involve:

- producing quarterly and/or annual profit and loss statements;

- developing interactive skills – helping others prioritize, communicate, innovate and become effective team players.

Managing well is more than a skill, it's an art – not easily mastered, but infinitely valuable to an organization, an entrepreneurial group or a single individual. Good managers generate confidence in employees by demonstrating that they know how to take control of a particular situation, project or group of employees. They often teach others by the examples they set. Their validity and credibility as leaders become apparent in the way they manage themselves. Employees watch their bosses to see how they deal with the four big testing-grounds of a manager's mettle – how they:

1. set goals;

2. deal with emotions;

3. handle stress;

4. manage time

Managing yourself

To learn how to manage yourself more effectively, start by reviewing your objectives. Once these are clear, it's easier to identify any problems you may have that interfere with managing your boss.

First, stop thinking of your work responsibilities as duties. That concept implies you're a passive worker waiting to be handed your next assignment. Show your boss you're an active, take-charge person. Start by thinking in terms of objectives, which aren't the same as duties. Objectives are goals – guideposts along the road you've taken – which you need to assess over the short and long term. Once these objectives are clear, share them with your boss. Ask for feedback. Make sure you both clearly see the direction in which you're heading. Once your boss knows you're serious about self-management, he'll be less likely to bother you with petty supervisory tactics.

Begin managing yourself by following these four steps:

Step 1.   Define objectives, measure performance

Start by writing down your personal and work-related objectives in one column and how you will achieve these objectives in another column. Performance measurement should include short-term (daily or weekly) and long-term (monthly, annual) evaluations. Your page might look something like this:

> *Objective.*   Improve participation and productivity during staff meetings. Build a greater sense of team spirit.

> *Action.* Communicate the purpose of meetings more clearly by providing detailed agendas. Seek feedback from participants and boss.

> *Monthly evaluation.* Better attendance, more informed discussion during meeting.

> *Annual evaluation.* Department morale higher, better team spirit.

2.   Prioritize responsibilities

Another effective management tool is learning how to prioritize. Managers rarely have responsibilities or projects that don't overlap.

Write down everything you do over a week's time, then take a look at tasks which are routine, yet time-consuming. If possible, delegate these tasks. Opening the post, for instance, and tagging the important correspondence can usually be handled by a secretary or an assistant. No matter how few employees you have to rely on, whether it's a word-processing department or someone else's assistant you've borrowed, you can always delegate a certain number of tasks. Ask yourself how many of the duties in the list below could be accomplished by an employee:

1. Return less important telephone calls.

2. Compose standard memos.

3. Proofread documents done by word processing department.

4. Prepare conference-room for meetings: supply clients with writing supplies, agendas, etc.

If delegating to an employee is not an option for you, try handling your mundane tasks in less time-consuming ways:

● *Combine tasks.* Open post while returning phone calls, placing conference calls.

● *Plan ahead.* When preparing a conference-room will interfere with other more important tasks, assemble supplies beforehand.

- *Just say 'no' – politely.* If your boss asks you to interrupt important work to do a less important task, find a diplomatic way to make him/her see your priorities your way. (Usually your priorities support your boss's so remind him/her of your *mutual* priorities.) Offer to do the other task later.

By prioritizing, your boss will get the picture that you have work under control, be impressed by your professionalism.

Learn to look at the big picture and decided what's really important for you to do for your boss. The higher your boss rises in the company, the more he or she will be deluged with trivial paperwork. You can free your boss's energy to do what he/she is best at by keeping your eye on your targeted professional objectives. Some of these may be to:

- consistently complete tasks and projects on time;

- when possible, learn to disseminate information through group meetings rather than numerous meetings with individuals;

- establish a relationship with a mentor. This could be your boss (see Chapter 9 on 'Good Bosses';)

- take the initiative when you see work that needs to be done or problems that need to be solved. (Don't wait for your boss to point them out);

- advertise your accomplishments by getting a story in the company newsletter or community publications.

By accomplishing these objectives in a proactive way, you'll not only position yourself favourably with your boss, you'll get a feeling for how he or she prioritizes objectives. You might even be able to help him/her prioritize.

Step 3.   Be flexible

Just as prioritizing is essential, it's also important to be flexible when changes occur. It may appear, at first glance, that your boss is incapable of making a decision and sticking to it. However, his/her actions could be determined by behind-the-scenes action of which you have no knowledge. Deadlines are often delayed and sometimes whole projects are abandoned while new ones are substituted.

When your boss tells you it's time to switch gears or directions, you can remain in charge by being flexible. Realize that it's the nature of things to change. Be able to accept new schedules, adjust your objectives and move forward actively. Your boss will appreciate you resilience. By accepting change you'll not only demonstrate your professionalism, you'll also make his or her job a lot easier.

Smart employees take advantage of the opportunities available to them during change to move
upward in their organization. Whether your company is undergoing a merger or your department is
getting new office furniture, show that you're able to
deal with delays and uncertainty. Don't rigidly cling
to old game plans. Instead, make up new ones. Seize
opportunities by being receptive to your boss's new
strategies. Even with a boss who frequently changes
his/her mind, don't throw in the towel. Throw your
support behind the new game plan, have fun with it
and plan to stick to it – until things change.

Step 4.   Becoming a team player, building trust

You may be on a team of one or 200, but being a
team player is what counts. The ability to co-operate
with others is the prime requirement for most jobs.
It shows your fellow office workers that you're not
playing the game to achieve your own ends but for
the good of the team. How can you build better
team skills?

First, whether you're managing employees or
simply managing yourself, make sure that group
goals and objectives are clearly defined and communicated. A corporate team is not much different
from a sports team. You might even find that your
boss has used some of the following football strategies in corporate team building:

1.   Perceive the goal.

2.   Devise a strategy on how to reach it.

3.   Motivate the team to do it.

4.   Prepare to counteract attempts to prevent it.

Keep in mind that one of your group's implicit goals is to forge better interpersonal relationships – a payoff of teamwork which builds mutual trust between employees and identification with the company. An important dynamic of interpersonal relationships is that the more an individual sublimates his or her individuality for the good of the team, the more that individuality is appreciated and acknowledged.

It's important for employees to know their bosses trust them to do their jobs without being overly supervised. Persuade your boss to assign open-ended tasks, he/she will be relieved of extra work and simultaneously demonstrate confidence in your ability to act independently.

Trust fosters better relationships both up and down the corporate ladder. It:

- encourages a better flow of information;

- allows greater creativity;

- promotes acceptance of individuals for who they are.

A good manager's job is very similar to a good parent's or a good coach's. A boss who is able to coach knows how much supervision employees require. And once a player knows the goal and game plan, a coach's job is to let go. A boss who is a good coach will let you carry the ball and win the game. Show trust in your boss to let you do a good job. And then do it.

Assessing yourself

Now that you know some of the basic management strategies, let's take a look at you.

Assessing your strengths, weaknesses, skills and strategies is one of the most difficult but productive exercises you can undertake to become a more effective manager of your boss. Having an objective understanding of who you are allows you to accept the parts you like and work on changing the ones you don't. It also makes it easier to separate your boss's constructive feedback from unwarranted criticism.

What are your goals?

Companies have mission statements; so should you. Take time to write down both long- and short-term goals. Start with the short-term goals because they will feed into long-term goals. Be as creative as you like. Don't limit yourself by defining goals which can be achieved only at your present job. Long-term goals can relate to work, family, hobbies and recreations – any part of your life you want to seriously develop. Your list could look something like this:

1. Improve my tennis.

2. Be a better mother, spend more time with my children.

3. Finish documentation project for new computer system at work.

4. Research family history.

5. Improve communication with my boss. Seek clarification of his expectations and identify a method of evaluation.

6. Write a romance novel.

7. Identify ways to become more innovative and demonstrate leadership at work.

8. Become my company's first woman director.

Now, prioritize the list. As much fun as writing a romance novel would be, chances are it's going to be outranked by finishing the documentation project at work. Yet spending more time with your children and husband is clearly an important consideration. Better time management and constant reprioritizing and delegating small tasks could free some time and energy to spend with the family.

Look for the fundamental issues: your commitment to your family; the need for advancement and recognition at work; a desire to take on a creative project; etc. It is important that you understand what issues are basic to your life and their priority. This understanding will help you resolve conflicts.

For instance, you are offered a promotion at work, but the new job requires a significant amount of travel. This means you would spend much less time with your children. What do you do? Do you accept or decline the job? The answer depends on the way you've structured your priorities. Here is a series of questions you can ask yourself to help resolve family/career conflicts:

1. What are my career goals?

2. How have they changed in the past few years?

3. What are my goals for my family?

4. How have they changed in the past few years?

5. Do my actions interfere with progress towards realizing these goals?

6. What elements in my life are in conflict with my career goals?

7. Is the position I currently hold really the best one for me?

8. Am I afraid of failing to meet my goals?

9. Am I afraid of meeting my goals?

10.　Am I prepared to adjust my career ambition?

These questions may prove difficult to answer,
but you will feel more comfortable with your decision if you've clearly defined and prioritized the
fundamental issues in your life.

Short-term goals are the stepping-stones whereby
you reach long-term goals. To achieve better communication with your boss and throughout the
department, you could set up monthly short-term
goals. For instance:

1.　Establish a method for passing on information to my boss. Make sure my boss is
passing on vital information to me that
has been received from management. If necessary, remind my boss that good communication allows both of us to do our jobs
better.

2.　When appropriate, schedule weekly meetings between staff and management to keep
projects on schedule.

3.　Solicit feedback from staff regarding the
effectiveness of meetings. Ask for ways to
help make their jobs easier. Is there training
or technical information they need? Are the
meetings helpful?

Now that you know where you're heading, let's
take a look at where you stand.

How do you fit in?

Consider your work habits. You may have just started in a new position or perhaps you've been at your job so long you could do your work in your sleep. Has the grind got to you or do you look at each day with its own set of challenges as uniquely different? Ask yourself the following questions:

1.   Am I dependable?

2.   Do I take pride in my work?

3.   Do I steer clear of destructive office politics?

4.   Do I try to learn from my mistakes?

5.   Do I approach problems as an opportunity to learn new skills?

Dependability means being at work on time, sometimes arriving early and staying late. Your behaviour sets an example to those both below and above you on the corporate ladder. Even a somewhat lazy and disorganized boss will improve their performance when they know they have conscientious, talented employees on their team who are prepared for meetings.

Pride in your work sends another clear message to your boss and colleagues. Working by the project, not by the clock, means that, if necessary, you're willing to dedicate time after work and on weekends to see that a project is done right and deadlines are met. No matter how long you've been in the same position, sloppiness and laziness are not acceptable.

If you feel your dedication is eroding, find new approaches to doing your job. You could:

- ask for training on new technology;

- job-share your present position with someone else in the company;

- attend a motivational seminar;

- find out how people in similar positions innovate in their jobs;

- explore the possibility of using your knowledge and experience to train for a new job within the company.

Above all, steer clear of harmful office politics – spreading malicious gossip and rumours. When you're in a managerial position, office rumours can be an important way of obtaining information you may otherwise be denied. But it's crucial to keep a professional attitude, to be supportive of fellow workers, especially your boss.

Summary

In this chapter we've examined some ways you can assess your own performance in the workplace.

To better manage yourself, you've learned how to:

- define your objectives;

- prioritize those objectives by delegating unimportant tasks;

- be a team player;

- develop short- and long-term goals;

- evaluate how you fit in with your work environment.

4

Emotions, time management and stress: three obstacles to managing your boss

Emotions, time management and stress can seriously derail your efforts to effectively manage your boss. How you overcome them will have a lot to do with how effectively you interact not only with your boss, but with co-workers and your employees. Ask yourself the following questions:

1. Do I become irritated over poor planning and tight deadlines?

2. Are relationships with my colleagues and boss complicated by unresolved issues in my life (insecurity, need for approval, conflicts with authority, for instance)?

3. Do I have the resources to get the job done right?

4. Am I constantly battling stress?

No matter how professional your demeanour or great your expertise, if you answered 'yes' to any of the above questions, chances are you could be alienating your boss.

Let's take a look at the three monsters that eat away at the most valuable resource any manager has: self-esteem.

Emotions

How many times has this happened to you? A boss whom you respect highly suddenly loses all control one afternoon and pounds a fist on the desk, berating a trembling secretary. Or the boss you admire for his/her ability to function under pressure is distraught over a minor addition to their workload. Even if you empathized with the boss, this loss of control probably made you see him/her in a new light.

Emotions can be volatile or chilling. They can make us explode with anger or droop from depression. No matter what their nature, the effect of emotions on our energy is draining – whether it's through the volatile rush of a temper tantrum or gradual desensitization from guilt and fear.

It's best to know what kind of emotions you experience on a daily basis. See if any of the following statements describe you:

1. I hide or suppress my annoyance with others.

2. I am frequently bored.

3. I can't concentrate on my work.

4. I feel pressured from all directions.

5. I avoid involving others in decision making and planning.

6. When I become openly angry, I feel guilty afterwards.

7. I frequently worry about trivial matters.

If you answered 'yes' to any of the above questions, you may have problems handling one or more of these basic emotions:

● anger;

● joy;

● fear;

● depression;

● trust;

● anxiety.

Everyone feels these emotions with some degree of intensity. They're only a problem when they keep us from performing our jobs, whether it's as a good employee, effective parent or happy, fulfilled adult.

Anger and depression

Some emotions funnel naturally into others. Unexpressed anger can lead to depression; unexamined fear can result in a heightened level of anxiety. Your performance at work will improve – your whole life will improve – when you're aware of your feelings and know how to deal with them. If you answered 'yes' to statements 1 and 6 above, you're experiencing anger.

In a later chapter we'll examine how you can effectively manage and communicate your emotions. The purpose of this chapter is to make you aware of them.

Surprisingly, feelings are often controlled by thoughts. Negative thoughts lead to depression, just as fearful thoughts lower self-esteem. Learning to monitor your negative thoughts is the first step to getting control of your emotions.

If you were to ask most people if they are angry, they would probably deny it. But here are some symptoms of unacknowledged anger.

- tense, tight muscles;
- speaking in a loud voice;

- knot in stomach;

- nervous mannerisms;

- quick, shallow breathing;

- increased heart rate.

People can suppress anger and bottle it up or express it in uncontrolled outbursts; but either way, anger is a particularly potent emotion. Unfortunately, it can also lead to high blood pressure, migraines, ulcers, teeth grinding and depression. Unexpressed or poorly expressed anger can damage your relationship with your boss and fellow employees because they will sense your latent hostility and feel defensive. We decide whether to be its slave or master.

Your feelings of anger, particularly with your boss, might be justified. Perhaps you have a boss who likes to deliberately upset and frustrate employees. Take your 'emotional temperature' and see if you have any unresolved feelings of anger towards your boss. Try to be objective and determine if they're justified. If so:

1. Clearly point out to him what it is he's doing that causes your angry reactions.

2. Explore possibilities for change.

If your boss isn't willing to change his/her behaviour, you should devise ways to monitor your own reactions before they reach the boiling point by:

1. excusing yourself for a 'cooling off' period when discussions become heated;

2. staying in touch with your feelings and giving your boss feedback: 'It's difficult for me to follow your instructions when you shout'.

If your angry feelings towards your boss seem unjustified or out of proportion, chances are you're dealing with unresolved issues of anger from your childhood. To find out if your anger is chronic, ask yourself:

1. Do I lose my temper easily over unimportant trivialities?

2. Does my boss's behaviour remind me of the parent with whom I'm really angry?

3. Is my anger predictable, i.e. certain times of the day (after breakfast, after lunch) when blood sugar is low?

Find a professional who can help you deal with your anger. It could be getting in the way of your career. When your boss sees you as over-emotional and edgy, he/she will hesitate to trust you with important assignments. As much as your boss values your strengths and abilities, your volatile, unpredictable reactions might make you an undependable team player.

Depression is a feeling of sadness or grief. It can spring from unexpressed anger or stem from a particular event such as a death in the family or a failure at work. Often people admit they're 'angry' at a friend or family member who has died, leaving them to contend with life on their own.

Depression has few, if any, positive effects. It does tell you something is wrong. When you deny depression, preferring not to examine its cause, it can turn into chronic depression which lowers your energy level and makes you unable to function.

The most effective way to cure depression is to first identify what's causing it. That can be relatively simple if you are suffering from an isolated case of depression caused by a major change in your life (moving, divorce, illness, etc.).

However, if you are chronically depressed, identifying the source of your depression is more difficult. This type of depression can be driven by numerous complex emotions. Among them are:

- low self-esteem;

- feelings of insecurity;

- constant need for approval.

If you think you fall into this category of chronic depression, consider talking to a counsellor, psychologist, minister or similar professional who can help you identify and correct the source of your depression.

You may have the world's most empathetic boss – or you may not. But even a supportive boss gets tired of an employee who needs constant re-energizing to get the job done. Depression may cause you to feel like you're completely isolated; however, your energy level affects everyone with whom you work.

To work through your depression you may need extra sleep, more privacy and understanding friends. It's unlikely you'll find any of these at work. Make every effort to counter the effects of depression by:

- getting to work on time;
- being decisive;
- taking pride in your work.

Avoid denying your depression by becoming a workaholic. Just do your job. Your boss will appreciate your professionalism.

Joy and trust

Joy is, or should be, a very real part of our daily lives whether we experience it at home or at the office. Joy restores our energies and regenerates our view of the world.

We've looked at what kind of power good bosses have. One of them is the power of personality – the ability to inspire others with enthusiastic leadership. Managers who lack joy are not inspirational. They can even infect employees with their own defeatism. By the same token, listless employees can make their boss's job much tougher, if not impossible. The effects of joy in the workplace are limitless. It can:

- motivate workers to participate in consuming, goal-oriented work;

- promote sharing, generosity and teamwork;

- allow workers to substitute the pleasures of discovery for the dull patterns of habit and routine.

How many times have we heard that it's important to find joy in our work? Your only joy in your dull job may come at five o'clock on Friday afternoon when you're free of the office for a weekend. If this is the case, you need to evaluate what you're doing and see if you can find a way to improve your job or move on to something more fulfilling. If your outlook is decidedly joyless, it may mean your self-esteem is at an all-time low. Here are four ways to boost it:

1. Avoid comparing yourself to others. Your achievements and abilities are unique.

2. Reward yourself.

3. Accept praise and accent the positive. Don't dwell on past mistakes.

4. Avoid self-criticism.

Joy fuels you with added energy. It allows you to work hard, acting with confidence and decisiveness, pushing projects through to their final conclusion.

Whether you love your job or simply find it pays the bills, every boss wants enthusiastic players on their team. Your joy and pride in your work can be infectious. They can enliven fellow workers and even a dull boss.

We've mentioned trust as a part of teamwork. We'll talk about it again in a later chapter on good bosses. Without trust, the corporate world would no longer exist. It's the glue that binds all relationships and agreements. Your trust in others can be limited by how much you trust yourself. Here are four ways to improve your self-trust:

1. View yourself as unique: don 't try to fit into a mould.

2. Listen to your inner voice.

3. Welcome responsibility.

4. Be spontaneous: follow your intuition in approaching a task or problem.

Self-trust gives you the following major advantages on the job:

1. It allows you to recognize and rely on your abilities.

2. It gives you confidence to cope with difficult situations.

3. It provides you with the inner strength to act decisively and push for results that may lack popular support.

If you find yourself relying too much on the rules, unwilling to delegate tasks, suffering from disorganization or supervising your employees' work too closely, you need to improve your trust in others and in yourself.

Trust begets trust. The more confident and self-trusting you are, the more you will trust your boss to do his/her job and your boss, in turn, will recognize your support by showing trust in *you*. Your boss will trust you to play by team rules, do the best job you can and handle difficult assignments. Mutual trust among employees and employers allows you to bypass time-consuming red tape, cumbersome rules and regulations. Once trust is established, both you and your boss will be more innovative, and your jobs will be more fun.

Fear and anxiety

Fear is one of the most basic emotions known to man. It prompts the body to pump adrenaline in anticipation of the classic 'fight or flight' situation. We experience fear almost daily, yet not many people would admit to being fearful. It simply doesn't go with the confident image demanded by the corporate world; yet we're all afraid of making mistakes, of displeasing our bosses, of losing our jobs.

Some people are afraid of not fitting in – of how business associates would regard them if they acted slightly different, or if their true natures were known. Some of those who have made it to top-level management jobs suffer from the impostor syndrome – they have constructed a professional persona that conforms to others' expectations.

A person in this situation may feel they have to be tough with employees to appear strong, or become a workaholic and forego spending time with their family to conform to a hard-driving executive image. Unfortunately, these people often think, 'This is not the true me. Somehow this all happened by accident. If others knew the true me I might lose respect, influence or power.'

When fear goes unexamined it can produce a high level of anxiety. Keep in mind it is an emotion that won't simply go away. To deal with fear effectively, you must recognize it then control it to your advantage.

When fear is out of control, it can limit your social and business life, and it can prevent you from functioning effectively.

Ask yourself the following questions:

1. Is fear limiting me in any way?

2. Do I frequently feel fearful?

3. Has my fear acted as a self-fulfilling prophecy on several occasions? If so, how?

Some fears are groundless, some are not. If you're afraid of displeasing your boss, try to ascertain if you're acting out of insecurity or if you have some reasonable motive. Perhaps your boss became openly hostile and punitive to other employees who displeased him in the past.

To overcome fear, it helps to rationally identify what you are afraid of, then think of a worst-case scenario. Make a realistic evaluation of what is liable to happen. Your list could look something like this:

Fear. Making mistakes at work.

Effect. Being ridiculed.

Worst outcome. I become angry, lose control, lose colleagues' respect at work.

Realistic evaluation. Everyone makes mistakes. Reasonable mistakes are generally tolerated where I work. I can learn from my mistakes.

Believe it or not, fear has positive uses in the business environment – it all depends on intensity and duration. Moderate, occasional fear stimulates; tremendous fear paralyses. People are most fearful when they're learning a new job or defending a present one. You can benefit from occasional fear in two ways:

1. It allows you to learn and evaluate new situations quickly.

2. It can stimulate you to develop effective countermeasures.

One way to conquer fear is through bio-feedback techniques: learn to relax, visualize yourself in a positive situation and make positive affirmations. Nothing can do more damage to your work performance than being afraid of your boss. You have to ask yourself if your fear is justified or misplaced. Does your boss bully and threaten employees or does your insecurity with your boss's ego make you uneasy?

Some bosses like throwing employees off-centre by behaving inconsistently, making unreasonable demands and alternately punishing or rewarding them at inappropriate times. Whatever your boss's behaviour, ask yourself:

1. Does my boss have anything to gain by making me afraid of them?

2. What do I have to lose by being afraid of my boss?

Unless your boss is violent, vindictive or deviant, chances are he or she is testing to see how far you will let them go with their 'obnoxious boss' act. If you think your boss's bark is worse than their bite, try standing up to them. Fear of your boss is a major hurdle for you to overcome. Tell them how their behaviour makes you feel; that you'd prefer them to monitor it when you're around. Your boss might not change, but they'll respect you for having the nerve to confront them.

If however, your boss's bite is worse than their bark, you've got a tough boss to handle. See the section on 'Tough, angry bosses' in Chapter 8.

Anxiety produces feelings of uneasiness and apprehension. Anxiety can result when you are worrying about a future event rather than confronting a present danger. Many people experience anxiety in the following stress-related situations:

1. Time pressures to work more quickly.

2. Evaluation of your work by an employer.

3. Increasing demands or complexity of your job.

4. Learning new skills.

5. Health problems.

6. Inner conflicts between personal values and job responsibilities.

7. Coming into contact with a large number and/or variety of people.

8. Getting a new job or a new boss.

People experience anxiety when they have to make changes. However, many times these changes are positive. Anxiety can have positive effects in the workplace. It can, for instance:

- motivate you to attack a problem directly;

- help you analyse a situation;

- prompt you to set goals, re-evaluate your talents and abilities, etc.

In addition, you may have to learn a few more skills in order to decrease your anxiety level, such as becoming more assertive or learning relaxation techniques.

No boss likes to work with a worrywart. If your boss perceives you as being over-concerned with petty details or taking up his time whining and complaining, his or her trust in you will erode.

When your anxiety is justified – due to rumours, or the company's poor financial performance – ask your boss to verify the information you have. He or she may not be in a position to confirm or deny the bad news, but they'll appreciate you letting them in on the grapevine.

Emotional rescue

To get a better grip on your emotions, it's helpful to keep an 'emotional diary'. Write down what you felt each day, at what time and, if possible, what event, individual or circumstance triggered the emotion. Some emotions, like irritability or depression, are triggered by varying levels in blood sugar occurring just before or after meals.

Notice if a pattern starts to emerge. See if you're

easily upset by the success of others – in which case your self-esteem may need bolstering. Check to make sure that the constant headaches, fatigue, cold and flu you're battling with really aren't symptoms of depression.

Don't try to wrestle with these emotions on your own. If you're not pulling out of a depression or you can't get control of your anger, it's likely the problem goes back to subconscious patterns learned early in your life. Don't hesitate to seek counselling. When in doubt, go to an expert.

Time management

The second obstacle you may face is time management. When five o'clock comes, have you completed most of the day's objectives or do you stare at the clock, wondering where the time went?

Managing time effectively is one of the most valued skills you can possess. When you know how to structure your time, you show your boss you're organized and efficient. You also show him that you value time – both yours and his – and, as a precious resource, you won't waste it.

If organizing your time is a problem, ask yourself these questions:

1. Do I get projects done on time or are they continually late?

2.   Do I need to spend more than 40 hours a week in the office?

3.   Am I willing to forego breaks and lunches to meet a deadline?

4.   Is my work constantly interrupted by my boss, other colleagues, phone calls?

5.   Is there time at work I spend in personal conversation which could be limited?

6.   Does my boss dump extra work on me? Does he or she frivolously reassign projects and deadlines to suit their changing schedule?

7.   Is my style of time management compatible with my boss's style?

Time management strategies

The way you manage time says a lot about the way you manage other aspects of your life.

Do you arrive at work about 10 minutes late, wander into the lunch-room for coffee and catch up on the morning's gossip with co-workers?

Or do you arrive a little early, directed and focused, with a list of what you plan to accomplish?

Now ask yourself, if you were the boss, which kind of employee would you prefer working with?

Maybe you'd like to be more like the employee in the second scenario, but getting organized is a problem. Once you're seated at your desk, phones start ringing, people drop by to visit and the day has taken off on a direction all its own. Priorities take the form of crisis management.

One way of gaining control of your time is to make a 'To do' list either before or as soon as you arrive at work:

- Include high, medium and low priorities.

- Work on one project at a time. Don't begin several projects at once.

- Don't take on extra projects until everything on the 'To do' list is finished.

To avoid interruptions while working on your 'To do' list, try some of the following strategies:

- If you have an office door, shut it.

- Ask the people at the switchboard to hold your calls, or put your phone on 'Do not disturb'.

- When co-workers drop by to chat, explain you're busy, then set up a time when you can get back to them.

Time management and your boss

You and your boss's ideas of time management may be diametrically opposed. Perhaps you're highly organized and your boss prefers to work more intuitively. Styles don't matter as long as both of you manage to get your respective jobs done. What *does* matter is when your respective styles of time management interfere with one another's effectiveness.

Ask yourself if any of these scenarios fit your relationship with your boss:

Scenario 1

Your boss is a stickler for meeting deadlines and commits 50 to 60 hours of the working week to the office. You, on the other hand, enjoy spending time with your family, have outside interests and lots of friends at work.

You think your boss:

- is too hard-driving;

- should spend more time with his/her family;

- worries too much about job performance; he or she has his or her boss's support and can afford to relax more often;

- interferes too much with your work style; would like you to work from a 'To do' list every day.

Your boss perceives you as:

- spending too much time socializing at work;

- disorganized and unmotivated;
- lacking in company loyalty;
- not helping him meet his deadlines.

Scenario 2

Your working style is dedicated and effective, your boss's style is laid back. While you like to pre-plan projects and meetings, your boss takes each day as it comes. You've already planned the vacation you're taking a year from now, your boss may take next week off ... he/she isn't sure yet.
  You perceive your boss as:

- relying on you to organize him/her;
- irresponsible and lazy;
- lacking an overall game plan for the department;
- standing in your way of possible advancement.

Your boss sees you as:

- too rigid and obsessive about time planning;
- wanting to control him/her;
- ambitious and easily frustrated;
- organized, yet overbearing;

● not well liked by colleagues.

In both scenarios, differing attitudes about time management can lead to real conflict between employee and boss. You may be better organized than your boss – especially if your boss depends on personal power to strengthen his or her position. Some bosses expect their employees to be better time managers than they are. Learn how to offer your time management skills to your boss without alienating him/her. The overall goal is to build a strong team and become a better player.

Here are some time management tips:

1. Construct a time log for the hours you spend at work. Include the time it takes you to dress and drive to work. Try keeping a diary at work that records time in ten-minute segments. Time at work can be allocated to three types of activities:

    ● *fixed activities:* staff meetings, production reviews, administrative matters;

    ● *semi-flexible activities:* routine correspondence, meetings with customers, supervising employees;

    ● *variable activities:* items beyond your control – phone calls, visits, personal matters handled during work hours.

2. Once you know how your time at work is spent, compare it to your short-term goals

for the day, for the week. Recognize the link between activities and goals. Each time you undertake an activity, ask yourself the following questions:

● Is this activity leading me toward or diverting me from a larger goal?

● Is it possible to combine activities so that I can free up bigger blocks of time?

Stress

Stress is part of daily life and it can become a serious obstacle. Driving in heavy traffic can produce stress; so can winning a marathon. Many high achievers find pleasure in the slight buzz they experience from so much to do in so little time. It's important to remember that stress can be caused by too many problems or too much success. Either way, your body interprets it as an overload of stimuli and responds by telling the adrenals to kick into high gear.

Stress, when not handled properly, can quickly escalate through various stages, beginning with anxiety and ending in a tonal inability to function. At this last stage, stress is your body's way of just saying 'no' and it means it.

Stress in the workplace often occurs when you take on too much. You feel it's your job to solve not only your own problems but those of your boss and staff as well. Yet despite an overloaded schedule, overwork will not kill you. Recent studies indicate that stress can limit your life expectancy only when you don't experience enough joy in your accomplishments.

Look at what you do. Evaluate how stressful your job is. Think about the issues involved in the discussions on emotions and time management. Unresolved emotional conflicts or poor time management can also add to your level of stress.

Keep in mind that the groups with the highest level of stress are not over-stretched directors or hard-pushed entrepreneurs – they are clerical workers. The reason? They have very little control over their working lives. At the bottom of the corporate ladder, they are subject to the whims of various bosses, personnel departments and warring corporate factions in need of their services.

To assess the built-in stress of your position, ask yourself the following questions:

1. Is my job stressful within itself (i.e. high pressure to perform, to meet deadlines)?

2. Do I make it more stressful than it need be?

3. Does my boss make it more stressful than it need be?

4. Do I have any personal power in this position?

5. How many bosses must I please?

6. Am I meeting overall goals in this position?

How does stress affect my relationship with my boss?

Even if you and your boss see eye-to-eye, stress still affects your working relationship. See if any of these situations fit:

- Your boss loads you down with plenty to do but, after you've met tough deadlines, fails to recognize your accomplishments.

- Your boss increases your responsibilities, but doesn't give you the resources (position or staff) to accomplish them.
- Your boss explains that you need to manage time more effectively, then derails you in a series of lengthy, pointless meetings.

'Joyless' stress comes from feeling disenfranchised, powerless and burdened with tasks. The more you take control of your life and say 'no' to a demanding or unenlightened boss, the more stress-free you'll feel. It will also make you better able to interact with your boss and those around you.

There's a bad kind of stress and a good kind. You and your boss may both be the kind of workaholics who bask in the glow of a demanding but rewarding working relationship. See if you two share any of the following kinds of 'good' stress:

- passion and enthusiasm for your work;

- being centred in the present, refusing to dwell on past successes or failures;

- mutual resourcefulness; drawing on each other's ability to constructively and imaginatively accomplish goals and create solutions.

- Personal power – your boss has the power to influence the environment; in turn, your boss empowers you;

- perseverance – a mutual commitment to innovation;

- optimism – you're both open to new options and share them as often as possible;
- goal-setting – you're both good at defining specific goals to be accomplished within specific timeframes.

Learning to effectively manage your emotions, time and stress is the first step in effectively managing your boss. It shows your boss you mean business and can control stress, without letting it control you.

Summary

In this chapter we've looked at possible obstacles to achieving your goal of managing your boss: emotions, time management and stress.

1. *Emotions.* We identified six key emotions and

how you can deal with them: anger, depression, joy, trust, fear, anxiety.

2. *Time management.* Becoming a better manager of your time shows your boss you're organized and efficient. You can implement various strategies to help gain control of your time:

● keep a 'To do' list with high, medium and low priorities;

● avoid interruptions: phone and personal.

Assess how you and your boss react to the concept of time management. Are your working styles the same or different?

Keep logs of how time is spent at work. Start linking activities to goals. Divide time into three kinds of activities: fixed, semi-flexible and variable.

3. *Stress.* Stress is how your body responds to too much stimuli. Its sources can be pleasant or unpleasant events, all signifying change of some sort.

See how you and your boss create stress for one another. Is it good or bad stress? Is some of it avoidable through better planning, better communication?

5

Get smart – get to know your boss

Knowing yourself is half the battle of managing your boss. Knowing your boss is the other half.

Hardly anybody really likes having a boss. In many cases the relationship all too closely mirrors the kind of relationship we had with our parents. Bosses tell us what to do, criticize our work, prioritize our tasks and time, and ultimately decide our future with the company. It's easy to fall into the trap of responding to our bosses the way we did to our parents: like over-compliant 'good' kids or sullen, rebellious teenagers. Neither kind of behaviour earns us a boss's trust. No matter how gruff or intimidating a boss may be, the last thing they need is an apple polisher or a terrorist. A good boss welcomes strong employees who aren't afraid to tell them when a problem exists. How that relationship develops is mostly up to you.

The first step in managing your boss is to realize your boss is fallible, a human being just like you, with measurable strengths and weaknesses. In this chapter we'll put all the interpersonal dynamics aside and take an objective look at your boss. You'll get to know him or her – maybe for the first time. You'll learn what your boss's needs are; and in the next chapter, you'll learn how to make your boss need you – a guaranteed prescription for a long and healthy career.

To get to know your boss better, assess their:

- goals;
- power;
- particular strengths and skills;
- ways of handling their emotions and those of others;
- way of handling stress;
- needs;
- personality and behaviour outside the office.

What are my boss's goals?

You spent some time in the first chapter defining and prioritizing your goals and objectives. Think how much those goals said about you – where you're heading, what you ultimately want from your career, your family, your life. What if you could take a look at a similar list of your boss's goals? It would tell you a lot about the person you're working for.

Ask your boss if he/she is willing to share a list of work-related goals and strategies with you, both short-term and long-term. Your boss may not even have defined them for him/herself. Or they may prefer to rely on a less structured approach – by verbalizing goals in project meetings.

Even if your boss is reticent about communicating his or her goals, you probably are familiar with some of them from your day-to-day contact. List the projects your boss is in charge of; also think about where he/she wants to go in the corporate structure. Then make a list of goals. Include what you perceive are commitments to family, religious community and favourite recreations. Don't worry about putting them in any particular order. It's more important to rely on your intuition and spontaneity in this exercise. Your list might look something like this:

My boss's goals

1. Get marketing project in on time and under budget.

2. Find a way to deal with frustration.

3. Keep his/her boss satisfied and off their back.

4. Spend more time with his/her children.

5. Arrange to spend more time with his/her partner.

6. Develop a modified projection of sales for the next quarter based on sales figures from branches.

7. Successfully present the new quarterly projection to his/her boss.

8. Help start a Neighbourhood Watch group.

9. Be under consideration for the marketing director position.

When your boss's goals are in conflict

One common source of boss–employee friction is when your boss has goals that conflict with one another.

If appropriate, check the above list with your boss. Be tactful and diplomatic, and limit your discussion to business goals. (Your boss probably won't be comfortable discussing personal and family goals with you.) By reviewing the list and using your intuition and observations regarding personal and family goals, you'll be able to spot the problem areas: weekends of number-crunching to project next quarter's sales will eat up valuable time your boss wants to spend with the family. What kind of additional responsibilities does your boss have? Is he or she willing to make further sacrifices of time and energy with two small children at home?

We'll tell you how to communicate solutions to these conflicts in the next chapter.

What kind of power does my boss have?

Review the power pyramid in Chapter 1 and see where your boss fits in. Ask yourself what kind of access your boss has to the following resources:

- increased budget for staff or supplies;
- time to devote to company planning;
- powerful allies in high places.

Getting a clear picture of what kind of resources your boss actually has gives you a more practical understanding of what he or she can do for the employees.

Now look at the six kinds of power outlined in Chapter 2. Evaluate what kind of power your boss brings to their relationship with you and to what degree.

The power of the position

The power to reward

Is your boss in a position to give you a promotion or

a raise? If so, is it only during an annual review or can he confer immediate raises and bonuses?

How does your boss recognize you for a job well done?

- *Informal recognition* – word of mouth, taking you out to lunch.

- *Formal recognition* – company newsletter, memo to others, including you in meetings and seminars.

- *Mentoring* – an acknowledged commitment on their part to take you under their wing to develop your promotability.

The power to punish

Does your boss have the power to fire you?

Does he or she have the power to redefine your job responsibilities or transfer you to another department?

Does he or she have the capability of undermining you so you'll quit? For example, by:

- subverting your authority over your employees;

- undermining your support from other bosses within the company;

- damaging your credibility by assigning you dead-end or problem projects.

The power of authority

Does your boss's authority come with the position? How effectively does he or she use it? Are they:

- Authority*philic?* Does your boss love exerting authority and over-running his or her bounds?

- Authority*phobic?* Is your boss afraid to claim it; does he or she run the risk of losing it?

Personal power

Expertise

Is your boss an expert at a particular function: marketing strategy, computer programming, architectural engineering?

Does your boss share his knowledge readily with others?

Is your boss grooming someone to take his place?

Does your boss expect you to easily grasp what only he or she understands?

Is your boss willing to teach you?

Referent power

Does your boss possess a tremendous amount of charm, charisma and integrity that makes others want to be like him or her?

Is your boss well-known and well-liked through-out the company, community and city?

Does your boss rely solely on charm to get others to do his or her job?

How does your boss interact with friends and family? In the same manner or differently?

Can your boss's connections help you get where you want to go?

Association

Does your boss 'come from the right family' or know the right people?

Does your boss's social background help or hinder in doing their job well?

Does your boss overlook your strengths because you're not from the same background?

Did your boss marry the boss's daughter/son, is he/she the boss's son/daughter?

What are my boss's strengths and weaknesses?

Make an honest appraisal of your boss's strong and weak points. Maybe you've been so overwhelmed by his/her charismatic personality that you've never stopped to realize that he/she is a little short on technical skill. Bosses, just like other people, need help in the areas where they're weakest. If your boss really knows how to motivate staff but lacks ability to follow through, he/she may need some organizational help.

Start observing your boss in action and keep a list of how he or she innovates, operates and motivates others – a kind of report card you can update regularly. Remember, the objective is not to indulge in excessive fault-finding but to see your boss in a new light – as a multi-faceted human being. Ideally, you'll discover a way to lend your boss a hand, make him/her look better and forge a stronger working relationship.

Your evaluation could look something like this:

Perceived strengths

- Manages time efficiently
- Good listener.
- Fair-minded.
- Good technical background.
- Has integrity.
- Defends his employees.

Perceived weaknesses

- Doesn't use all the resources available to the department.
- Too detail-minded, loses sight of the big picture and long-range objectives.
- Not perceived as a strong leader within the company.

By comparing what you perceive to be your boss's strengths and weaknesses, you'll get a good feel for where he or she's effective and where they could use some help. The above individual has a lot of technical expertise and is a caring, loyal boss who supports his employees. He or she is not a charismatic or skilful enough corporate player to claim much of the company's resources, such as a bigger budget for more computer terminals, additional staff or raises. Chances are, their most ambitious employees will want to work for a more powerful supervisor in a department where the stakes are higher.

It's important to realize that *your* attitude can enhance both your boss's strengths and his weaknesses. Remember, all bosses are judged by how well they perform for their immediate superiors *and* how well they motivate their employees. That's where you come in. Eventually, you'll learn how to help your boss improve their performance. But the best way to start is to show them you're on their side, that you're playing on their team – a team that will make you both winners.

My boss, my coach

If part of your childhood wasn't spent in the competitive world of team sports, there might be some confusion as to what being on a team is all about. Being a team player means the following:

- your ultimate loyalty is to the team;

- you carry out your role or assignment as expected;

- you are willing to set aside your desires and wishes for the good of the team;

- once you're in the game, the time for debate is over;

- all team members must play as a team.

If you have played a childhood game or sport as part of a team, you soon learn the essentials of play from a good coach.

- Winning and losing aren't as important as playing well.

- There's always the next game.

- Rules are important; they're what you play by.

- By playing, you're constantly improving.

- Team mates are bound together by a higher good that overcomes individual differences.

Maybe your boss is the greatest coach ever. Or maybe he/she has never set foot on a playing field. What's important is your boss's ability to be a leader, to improve the performance of his or her employees and to inspire trust. To find out if your boss is a good coach, ask yourself the following questions:

1. Does my boss understand the game?

    ● Does my boss communicate goals well?

    ● Does my boss have an effective game plan?

    ● Is my boss flexible; can he or she change game plans when necessary?

    ● Is my boss fair – does he or she play by the same rules they expect us to play by?

2. Does my boss understand the team?

    ● Does my boss perceive and use each team member's strengths and talents?

    ● Does my boss trust us to win?

    ● Does my boss inspire us?

    ● Is my boss consistent?

    ● Does my boss empower us?

    ● Does my boss test our abilities by giving us difficult roles to play?

    ● Does my boss reward us?

And, finally, the most important question:

3. Does my boss make it fun to play on his/her team?

- Do team members enjoy playing on my boss's team?

- Do others want to play on this team?

Being a good coach doesn't mean having all the answers. Good bosses solicit feedback from employees. It shows they respect their employees' opinions and trust them to be truthful. Evaluate how receptive your boss is to the two basic types of feedback: positive criticism and helpful suggestions.

1. Can you openly discuss problems with your boss?

2. How does your boss respond when you make suggestions? Does he or she:

   - thank you for your concern;

   - deny your feedback;

   - defend themself?

3. Does your boss accept feedback only from immediate superiors?

4. Does your boss relay performance feedback to you:

   - directly, through meetings or performance reviews; or

- indirectly, through other employees or departments?

How my boss deals with emotions

Your boss's team-building ability can be affected by the way he or she handles emotions. The facts of life apply at the office as well as at home: people are full of human frailties. Disguise it as they might behind tough facades or curt communication, bosses – like employees – have to deal with the emotions that arise as a result of failure. Evaluate your boss in the following areas:

1. *Keeping a positive mental attitude.* Perhaps your boss failed once and is too afraid of failing again to really try.

2. *Separating the process from the product.* If your boss's strategies were good but the effort failed, it might not be his or her fault.

3. *Avoiding perfectionism.* The workplace is full of distractions and conflicting priorities that call for compromise and doing the best job possible, then moving on. Don't dwell on how much better a project could have been.

4. *Learning to value failure.* Growth and discovery can't take place without failure. Learn to live with it as a fact of life.

5. *Trusting and empowering employees.* They're here to learn how to do their jobs. The better they are, the better the boss's entire department or product will be.

Depending on how well your boss deals with their own emotions, he or she may fall into an emotional type: angry, effective or fearful. See if any of the following situations sound familiar.

The angry boss

Some bosses use anger as a means of controlling others – especially their employees. To this person, the advantages of bullying tactics far outweigh the disadvantages that may result from losing control.

Obviously, no one wants to bring an angry boss bad news. Inappropriate anger by a boss shuts down communication with employees and transforms employees from supportive to subversive overnight. When your boss is extremely frustrated, an angry outburst may be justified and can even be healthy. The key is: does your boss express anger appropriately and constructively? Does your boss play fair? Ask yourself the following questions:

1. Does your boss keep his or her remarks impersonal: focused on an action and not personal characteristics?

2. Does your boss refer only to the situation at

hand and not dwell on the past, reciting old infractions and mistakes?

3. How does your boss react to an angry employee?

4. Does your boss check the facts to make sure his or her anger is directed at the right person?

5. Does your boss give someone a chance to explain before getting angry?

6. Does your boss make it clear why he/she is angry?

7. Does your boss make threats?

8. Does your boss provide alternatives or solutions?

9. Does your boss chastise employees in private or in front of their co-workers?

Being the object of another person's wrath – especially when it's your boss's – is upsetting and frightening. Try to stay objective and see if your boss has a valid reason to be upset.

Some tough, overly-aggressive bosses allow no room for error. If this is your boss's style (which is to say everyone is treated this way), it's important not to take an outburst personally. It helps to try and ascertain the underlying motive for your boss's behaviour. Some possibilities are that they:

- believe in the 'drill sergeant' approach to motivating others;

- have a strong need to control and intimidate others;

- are highly emotional; in other words, their enthusiasm is as intense as their negativism.

To see if you're reading your boss right, watch how he/she interacts with other employees and with superiors.

The effective boss

The effective boss has his or her emotions under control but is not afraid to display them when appropriate. He or she knows that without emotions, a corporate environment is dull and sterile. Emotions can be used positively to motivate employees, build empathy and foster team spirit.

Effective bosses are willing and able to co-ordinate plans, programmes and people with intelligence and understanding. They let employees know where they stand and guide the department to meet its goals and get the job done within the limitations of budget, staff or policy decisions.

To find out if you are working for an effective boss, ask yourself:

1. Do my boss's successes outnumber his or her mistakes?

2. Does my boss handle failure realistically and move on to the next project with confidence?

3. Does my boss avoid over-supervising his staff?

4. Is my boss truly concerned with his employees' happiness?

5. Does my boss's department make money?

6. Does my boss expect the same high-level performance from him/herself as from his or her employees?

7. Does my boss recognize and reward employees who have performed well?

Effective managers are good psychologists, using the varied emotional make-up of their employees to enhance their department. They know when to support employees who lack confidence, when to bend the rules for employees going through a difficult family crisis, when to give ambitious employees a chance to show what they can do. An effective boss prizes, above all, individual talents and abilities and knows that a happy staff will require less direct supervision, allowing him or her to explore and develop their own strengths.

The fearful boss

Weak bosses often fear their own bosses and envy employees who appear more confident than themselves. A weak boss can sabotage you just as easily as an over-aggressive boss. Rather than ignoring weak and fearful bosses and hoping they'll just fade away, it's best to take the initiative and work with them. Try to find out why they're the way they are. Maybe they have just cause. Your slightly insecure boss could have been beaten down over the years by a bullying superior. Maybe all your boss lacks is confidence. You can help your boss become more emotionally secure by giving positive feedback and encouragement.

Ask yourself if your boss has problems with any of the following:

- working well with their immediate superior (i.e. fearful of not pleasing their boss);

- working well with employees (i.e. fearful they're going to steal their job);

- not a good team manager;

- lacking in management training; promoted because of their expertise;

- handling a new position that has duties they are unfamiliar with;

- learning from past mistakes and not dwelling on them;

- willingness to take risks.

A fearful boss may want to minimize conflict at

any cost, not realizing that incompetence can undermine employees as quickly as bullying tactics.

Establishing the proper balance with your boss between aggressive yet productive interaction is of importance to employees and superiors alike.

What is my boss's personal style?

Your boss's personal style can say more about him/her than their list of goals. It is after all, the way your boss wants the rest of the world to perceive them. First, look at your boss's style of communication. Is it formal or casual, preferring written memos to verbal messages or the reverse? A 'paper person' likes to have information communicated first in readable form, followed by a personal talk. 'People persons' are just the opposite, relying on meetings followed by detailed written reports. It's important to understand that your boss's style of communication is based on how they process information. So if your boss is paper oriented, send him/her a memo, even if you hate adding to the departmental paper-chase. And if your boss is people-oriented, don't hesitate to set up a short meeting to discuss new information.

Styles of management

Your boss's management style may be the product of a self-image that thrives on flamboyance and fun.

Does your boss see himself or herself as an adventurer, charting the unknown seas of corporate enterprise? Does he or she give free reign to their imagination in tackling problems? Chances are, if your boss is innovative and gifted, he or she allows employees the same kind of creative leeway. If this is the case, you couldn't ask for a better boss. A daring and original leader, if allowed plenty of developmental latitude within the company, will recognize your inner resources and know how to make use of them.

A boss's style can often be shaped by their profession. Bosses who have served in the military, worked in law firms or government bureaucracies tend to be more formal, rigid and fond of doing things 'by the book'. A militaristic boss will emphasize the importance of the chain of command, reporting all matters to your immediate supervisor and following orders without undue questioning.

A boss's management style can change – particularly when, as an entrepreneur, they have more personal freedom of expression. When small companies undergo rapid financial growth, your boss's style may also undergo a change – from a freewheeling small-business owner to a more corporately correct managing director, ready to interact with directors of other successful businesses.

Preferred lifestyles

Evaluate, if you can, what your boss is like outside

the office. You could be in for a big surprise. The ogre that has everybody trembling before a staff meeting could transform into an adoring parent at the sight of their two-year-old toddler.

It's always heartwarming to see a boss who's been cold and reserved at work exhibit warm feelings for family and friends. You know that he or she has a life – a happy life – outside the office. The reasons for their hard-driven behaviour at work become apparent. Your boss suddenly makes more sense to you in ways they never did before.

A boss's interests and recreations say a lot about them. Does he prefer reading to tennis? Opera to rock music? Fishing to racing-car driving? And who does he share these enthusiasms with?

How your boss chooses to relax tells you about the other side of his/her personality. You might be surprised to learn that the stern disciplinarian you work for Monday to Friday is passionately fond of gardening and is an amateur archaeologist. Differences in personality can be obliterated if you discover you and your boss share a common interest, volunteer for the same community group or belong to the same church. Suddenly, the boss you found so offensively loud and overbearing becomes more human. It helps to know that the person who demands those reports from you on Friday afternoon is the same one who coaches their daughter's swimming team. It's easier for employees to work for bosses who, like them, have commitments to family, outside interests and community groups that expand and enrich their lives.

What are my boss's needs?

Every boss has certain basic requirements to sustain life within the corporate world. Bosses aren't omniscient or infallible. They need subordinates who will support them, keep them informed and, above all, intuitively understand their needs.

Some of your boss's needs are universal, others are specific to your particular boss. Every boss, for instance, needs subordinates who can be counted on for the following:

- loyalty;
- dependability;
- relaying vital information
- protecting the boss's time;
- sensitivity to pressures the boss is experiencing.

To truly understand the kind of pressure your boss is under, take a look at *their* boss. Is your boss's boss undemanding, fair and loyal? Does he or she willingly extend support to your boss's projects? Or are they a tough, aggressive line manager who views each department's contribution in terms of profit and loss? Maybe there's a lot your boss would like to do for his or her employees but simply can't because of budgetary considerations or a work style that differs widely from that of their own boss.

Companies undergo their greatest stress during periods of growth. So do bosses. If your company has recently undergone a merger, added new departments or changed its product line, try to evaluate what kind of pressure this creates for your boss. It's also stressful when companies shrink, cut middle managers' positions or get 'lean and mean' for the long fight ahead. If possible, keep abreast of market trends and financial markets – any general economic factor that could have an impact, directly or indirectly, on your boss.

Once you've gauged the kind of pressure your boss deals with daily, you'll have a better feel for the ways in which you can meet his/her needs as a high-performing team player.

Develop mutual trust

Trust, as an emotion, was discussed in Chapter 3. Your boss needs to trust you just as you need to trust him/her. Being a trustworthy employee means being loyal to your boss and being dependable. Your boss wants an employee who will:

- support their decisions;
- avoid political games;
- show up for work;
- do the work.

Your trustworthiness is the solid foundation of your relationship with your boss. You may exhibit talent, brains and blind ambition, but if your boss feels he or she can't trust you, you're going nowhere within the organization.

Share information

The kind of information you give your boss and the frequency with which you deliver it is up to your boss to specify. This kind of information sharing is usually done formally through meetings and memos.

But vital information doesn't always travel downward through the chain of command, nor is it formal in nature. Sometimes employees are privy to information their bosses never hear. You can effectively sabotage your boss by not sharing this information with them just as you can strengthen their position by filling them in.

Information is channelled through informal conversations, the rumour mill and shared group activities: parties, the office cafeteria (or rest room), bowling leagues, squash courts, country clubs, charity balls and bars. To separate what your boss needs to know from mere idle gossip, ask yourself:

● Is this information that affects my boss's position?

- Is this information that affects the future of the company?

- Is this information something my boss needs to know about an employee, a project or budgeting that could affect his or her decision?

Avoid being a tell tale, spy or office sneak. If your boss hears you spreading destructive gossip about co-workers or other bosses, they'll assume, by process of deduction, that you gossip in the same manner about them.

Protect his time

One of your boss's most valuable resources is time. The higher a boss goes in the corporate structure, the more demands are made on their time. Since your boss's effectiveness is measured by how well he or she accomplishes goals, it's up to you to help your boss plan time carefully. Don't waste it in unnecessary conversations, meetings or phone calls. When reporting to your boss, make sure your information is correct, concise and not unnecessarily detailed.

Don't take advantage of your boss's good nature. If your boss is someone who loves a good joke or indulges in mild banter, don't initiate such interactions when they're obviously pressured.

Effective time management was discussed in

Chapter 3. If you feel your boss could use some help organizing their own time, offer to help with 'To do' lists, understanding priorities and turning time-consuming one-on-one meetings into more efficient group meetings. But offer only when he/she is not busy.

Give him respect

And finally, never underestimate your boss. Even if you're convinced they're totally incompetent. You just might be wrong and that would be a terrible mistake to make.

Even if you overestimate your boss's abilities, you've made the right move because you've gained an important ally. To get anywhere within a company, almost everyone needs help from above – that means a boss who likes, trusts and respects you.

And what better way to move up than with a boss who's going places? You might as well make the trip first-class – for you both.

Summary

Bosses are human beings, just like the rest of us. Show your boss that you are willing to take the time to find out what they're all about. Learn about their goals and how to spot when they're in conflict.

Your boss has certain kinds of power: the power

of the position and personal power. How does he or she use it?

Assess your boss's individual strengths and weaknesses, how they handle emotion, their perceived work style, personal interests and recreations.

Finally, find out what your boss's needs are. What kind of stress is he or she under? What do they need from you as an employee? Learn how to be trustworthy, protect their time and relay vital information.

Observe the cardinal rule of all working relationships: never underestimate your boss. It's too expensive an error to make.

By understanding your boss's needs, you'll see him or her in their full perspective – and you might even win an important ally.

6

Meeting your boss's needs

Your one sure-fire ticket to increased job security, career advancement and graduating with honours from the School of Boss Management is to know your boss's true needs and then to work out how to satisfy them without, of course, compromising your own needs. In this chapter we'll look at how to meet your boss's needs by:

- doing your job and helping your boss do his/her job;

- Evaluating your boss's needs and deciding when they're legitimate, when they're not;

- resolving conflicts between your needs and your boss's.

Many bosses, like the rest of us, have never actually identified what their needs are. They think of needs in terms of jobs awaiting completion: messy projects, piles of paperwork or salary increases and promotions. Your boss may need help with his or her job and not even know it. Maybe you're just the person to compile those dull monthly reports or add some sprightly prose to their upcoming speech. The trick lies in getting them to acknowledge where they need help.

Meeting your boss's work needs

One of the most fundamental needs any boss has is the ability to rely on his employees to perform with competence and authority. This translates into you doing the following whenever possible:

- *taking the initiative* – performing necessary tasks without being asked to do them, being a 'self-starter';

- *solving problems* – not appearing helpless when confronted with a problem;

- *using resources* – making use of the expertise or knowledge available in other departments

(or outside your company) to get problems
solved and work completed;

- *not complaining* – identifying problems and
  discussing them constructively when appropriate;

- *asking questions when you don't understand* –
  being organized when you seek help. Pick an
  appropriate time to talk to your boss; explain
  the problem concisely; list your alternatives,
  if any, and specifically explain the type of
  help you need.

Remember, you boss is judged on how well *you*
perform. Therefore competence heads the list of
qualities you must possess to further your relationship with your boss.

Also, bosses expect their employees to display a
level of professionalism that is comparable to their
own. Demonstrate to your boss that when you are in
the office you are there to work and get the job done
in a professional, organized fashion. If your boss sees
you as someone who behaves professionally, is punctual, thorough and dependable, then you will gain
tremendous credibility and leverage – both of which
are essential in effectively managing your boss.

Your boss's unmet work needs

Another area where you can meet your boss's needs

is by helping out with work that needs to be done, yet isn't getting done. Your boss doesn't have time for it, and it's technically not part of your normal work assignment. You can offer to help your boss out with some of the work, but be careful how you approach him/her. Depending on their level of self-confidence or how much they trust you, your boss might interpret your action as an attempt to usurp his/her power.

One way to meet your boss's needs in this situation is to help him/her get a grip on their incoming paperwork. Especially if you excel at written communication and your boss is not particularly print oriented, you could offer to summarize longer reports and memos and verbally report on shorter ones.

Ask yourself if you can help your boss meet his or her work needs in any of the following ways:

1. When you have writing skills and your boss finds writing dull and demanding:

    ● Understand the core of what your boss wants to communicate, then write the longer memos and reports for editing and final approval.

    ● Ghost-write your boss's speeches.

    ● Proofread, edit and see that major bases are covered in inter-departmental communications your boss writes.

2. When you have organizational skills and your boss prefers to interact with people:

- Either put your boss on a schedule or ask him/her to share their schedule with you so you can make appointments when they're busy elsewhere. Confirm all appointments and changes with them at the end of the day.

- Introduce a new filing method or keep duplicate files of his/her work where you both have easy access to relevant projects.

- Convince your boss to restructure meetings so time is used more effectively. For instance, combine group meetings instead of holding numerous individual ones.

How effective you are in meeting your boss's needs is often determined by your approach. If your boss is open, enthusiastic and the two of you share a successful track record based on mutual trust and past accomplishments, you can be fairly open in your approach. Yet even the world's most confident boss doesn't like to be reminded of areas where they're weak. Keep the following guidelines in mind when meeting with your boss to offer your help.

1. Choose a time that's good for your boss –

when they're not distracted, depressed by bad news or in the midst of planning for another meeting.

2.   Begin by complimenting them on something they do well, 'Congratulations on the new contract you negotiated. No one else in this company could have handled it so well.'

3.   Remain upbeat. Think of positive ways to express the help you're offering and why you're offering it. Stress the benefits you'll each receive. 'I thought this would be good for both of us. Learning to prepare the monthly report would be a good learning experience for me and at the same time would free you to concentrate on more important projects that coincide with the report's monthly deadline.'

4.   Be open to your boss's suggestions. If they agree to turn over some of their work to you, they'll probably want to experiment on a project-by-project basis.

5.   Be discreet. Let your boss know you'll take on this extra assignment in confidence without advertising it to co-workers.

6.   Provide closure without pressure. If your boss agrees to think about your offer, close by giving feedback and proposing a deadline for a decision: 'We agree then that you'll let

me know your decision by next Wednesday?'
If your boss accepts your offer, but doesn't
provide structure, close by saying, 'Then
you'll get the report data to me by next
Wednesday and I'll give you a first draft by
Friday?'

When your relationship with your boss is less
open, you may have to approach him/her more
subtly. When they see that you're not only hard-
working and dependable but also possess a particular skill that they lack, they'll eventually find a way
to ask you for help in the form of 'offering a chance
to prove yourself.' In this case, accept graciously
and let your boss think it was his or her idea.

Here are some ways you can indirectly advertise
your skills to help your boss with his or her work
needs:

1.   Offer your services on a specific project to a
     lateral boss with similar needs as your boss.
     (But get your boss's approval first!)

2.   Ask your boss to send you to a seminar you
     want to take: on time management, business
     communications, etc.

3.   After a positive performance review, tell
     your boss you'd like more responsibility. Be
     specific. List what you can do. Can your boss
     think of a way to use your strengths?

And finally, be sure to distinguish between helping your boss meet his or her needs and becoming the unacknowledged 'power behind the throne' who writes their speeches, prepares their annual reports and compiles the agendas for their meetings – all without adequate recognition or compensation. If your boss begins thinking of you as a blindly loyal subordinate to whom he or she can entrust more and more work without recognizing and rewarding you, then it's time to update your job description and insist on a performance review.

Meeting your boss's emotional needs

Some bosses need to know they're liked by employees. Others act as though they couldn't care less. Maybe your boss is generous and fair but needs to see him/herself as a head of a family rather than as a departmental manager. No matter what kind of a boss you have, you can help him or her to be a better one by understanding their emotional needs and – when they're legitimate – meeting them.

Let's first identify some common emotional needs bosses have. See which ones fit your boss:

1. *Positive feedback.* Everyone needs to hear when they're doing a good job – even bosses. Give your boss a pat on the back now and then, particularly when he or she has distinguished him/herself by meeting difficult

deadlines, winning awards or promotions. Your positive feedback can mean a lot to your boss when they're going through a difficult time. Single out one of their better qualities – leadership, fairness, warmth – and let them know they're appreciated. Tell them you enjoy playing on their team.

2. *Loyalty.* You can show your loyalty to your boss by demonstrating good work habits – being punctual and focused – and by carrying out orders without undue complaining or questioning. Reserve criticism of your boss for a one-on-one meeting with him. Bosses need loyal, trustworthy employees. In turn, they should reward you by supporting you with upper-level management.

3. *Respect.* No matter how laid-back or fun-loving a boss you have, he or she still need your respect. A boss is never more vulnerable than in front of *their* boss or upper-level management. If you see that your boss has switched gears into a more structured, formal approach, do them a favour and follow suit. Don't persist in addressing your boss informally or casually dropping by his or her office.

By working out what your boss needs emotionally, you'll be fulfilling a subtle requirement that is never mentioned on a job description. When you meet your boss's emotional needs, he or she will rely on you, trust you, confide in you more than they would a more highly skilled but less empathetic co-worker.

Unreasonable emotional needs

Occasionally, bosses make excessive emotional demands on their employees and co-workers. Their actions are prompted by unresolved emotional needs that seem to percolate through a bottomless pit of insecurity and low self-esteem. Ask yourself if your boss possesses any of the following characteristics:

Uses an employee as an emotional crutch

This boss will use the intimacy that results from daily working relationships to establish an emotional dependency in which the employee becomes a substitute authority figure of the father/mother variety. At first, you may welcome what appears to be your boss's trust and confidence and eagerly respond with advice or interested observations. Eventually, however, the boss's dependency interferes with the work that needs to be done and you finally see that you are placed in a compromising relationship with your boss. Not only is it unprofessional, but emotionally draining as well. To back off may seem like career suicide, but to encourage such an exchange is equally harmful.

What you can do

Try to determine if your boss is going through a particularly difficult phase either in relation to career or at home. You might want to bear with your boss until the pressure eases off. If the behaviour seems to be neurotic, however, don't think twice about ending your involvement. Chances are, if you create some distance, your boss will find another sympathetic ear. Set limits on your time and the kind of topics you're willing to discuss. If you need to discuss business with your boss and he or she wanders off the subject, listen politely, then firmly bring him or her back to the subject. You can try nonverbal communication like looking at your watch, or simply say, 'Did we reach a decision about how we're handling the sales reports?'

Over-controlling

When your boss has to be involved in every decision, large or small, refuses to delegate and has trouble letting go of a project once it's near completion, they're exhibiting overly-controlling behaviour. No employee welcomes working with a boss who's continually peering over his or her shoulder, asking how it's going, substituting their way of doing things for your way. Work flow is interrupted, precious time is lost and employees are never given assignments through which they can prove themselves or better their skills. Oddly enough, what the over-controlling boss actually lacks is self-trust. His refusal to delegate only mirrors his lack of trust in himself.

What you can do

When your over-controlling boss is interrupting you for the tenth time, tactfully tell them you'll be happy to incorporate any of their suggested changes once you've completed the project.

Not open to suggestions/criticism

Your tough, intimidating boss may actually be hiding behind a facade designed to scare off employees who would offer unwanted suggestions. Behind those intimidation tactics lurks someone whose low self-esteem will not accept criticism of any kind – no matter how kindly it is offered. Bosses who feel psychologically powerless often try to intimidate their employees in an attempt to exhibit their control.

What you can do

There are no quick and easy solutions to repairing another person's wilting self-esteem. Well-deserved compliments are likely to go unheeded as are any other kinds of public recognition. You may experience a high degree of conflict with a boss who attempts to control through domination. No matter how angry you feel, try to remain in control of your reactions. Your over-intimidating boss isn't simply in search of a way to complete a task; he or she also wants a reaction. If you can give them the work they want minus the reaction, they'll take their upsetting tactics elsewhere. Try to become aware of where their self-esteem is lacking. Then look at ways in which you can honestly bolster it without being obviously manipulative.

The moody boss

A boss who goes through several mood changes each hour isn't necessarily making unreasonable emotional demands on you. They're simply at the mercy of their own emotions and can't help displaying them at inappropriate times. If your boss's spirits plummet from congeniality to black despair and back up again, keep in mind that their reactions aren't based on anything *you've* done.

What you can do

Rule number 1: don't take his reactions personally. Rule number 2: give him some feedback. Based on how open your relationship with your boss is, let him or her know how their psychological states affect clients, co-workers and upper management. It might be a behaviour they're not aware of and can change. Possibly, it's something they can't change. When dealing with a moody boss, timing and anticipation are the keys. Try to anticipate when they're most open, when they're not. When you have to bring your boss bad news, time your message carefully. You may feel like you're constantly walking on eggshells with this boss, but the payoff is worth it.

When your needs and your boss's needs conflict

What happens when your boss's needs infringe on your sense of what's appropriate and inappropriate, right and wrong?

When your boss's behaviour goes beyond obnoxiousness and becomes psychologically dysfunctional, resulting in sexual harassment, dangerous threats and illegal practices, you need to act swiftly and firmly. See Chapter 8 on bad bosses to find out what you can do.

Conflicts with bosses often arise from different styles of working. Consider yourself lucky if your work style meshes smoothly with that of your boss. Here are some typical examples of conflicting work styles:

Employee needs

- To work autonomously
- Spontaneous feedback/strokes
- To have freedom to be creative

Boss needs

● To be constantly involved and continuously supervise employees' work

● To remain aloof, protect his privacy. Views spontaneity as an informal style of management

● To control all aspects of work assignment.

In each of the above examples, employee/boss needs differ radically. As an employee, you have management theory on your side which stipulates that bosses need to be responsive to their employees' needs. Here are some steps you can follow to ensure that mutual expectations are met without either party feeling unduly compromised:

1. Evaluate how deeply ingrained your boss's work style is. How long has he or she held their position? Have they ever worked differently?

2. Do other employees feel the same way you do? A boss may be more likely to listen to five employees instead of one about the need for change.

3. Make sure you and your boss define mutual expectations. Be specific about what you need to work more productively.

4. Be willing to compromise.

Even if you're successful at negotiating only some small change in your boss's work style – say, initiating weekly staff meetings with an aloof boss – you've won a huge battle. It means your boss is willing to listen to what you have to say and make changes. Thank him or her for their co-operation and build an impressive track record with them. That way, next time a conflict of work styles arises, they'll know that making a change is worth the trouble.

Summary

In this chapter we've examined how you can meet your boss's work and emotional needs. Your boss's main need is to have employees he or she can rely on to do their jobs with competence and authority.

Your boss may also need help with his or her own work load from a talented employee. A great many unmet needs among supervisory staff are tasks requiring organizational and communication skills.

Your boss also has emotional needs. Some examples of legitimate emotional needs are: loyalty, respect and positive feedback. You may also feel that your boss's needs border on the unreasonable, stemming from unresolved emotional problems. If this is so, see if there are ways you can interact with your boss to protect yourself and make them aware of the inappropriateness of their requests.

By meeting your boss's needs you can demonstrate your competence to do the job while building their trust in you to meet their emotional needs.

When you and your boss's needs are in conflict, it's best to resolve problems by soliciting feedback on mutual expectations. Be clear about the changes you need from your boss to do a better job – then, when your boss accommodates your request, work hard to prove both of you right.

7

Building better communication with your boss

No matter how great a relationship you have with your boss, everyone can benefit from learning how to communicate more effectively, more efficiently and more clearly.

In this chapter we'll look at the following:

- communication habits you may want to break;

- how to communicate with your boss;

- nonverbal communication problems to watch for;

- how to communicate in writing.

Communication habits you may want to break

The following scenarios illustrate some cardinal rules which pertain to the way employees communicate with a boss. See if any of them sound familiar.

1. You tell all your friends what a great boss you have. It's almost like working for an older brother or sister, you can pop into their office any time to ask questions or just chat. They often drop by your desk to tell you about their latest date, then enquire as they're ready to leave, 'Hey, any problems with that last project I gave you?' Actually, you *do* have a few problems, but you hate to bring them up and ruin the great time the two of you are having.

2. You work for someone you really respect. Everyone in the company agrees that he/she are not only good, they're brilliant at what they do. They're published articles. They're even appointed by the mayor to serve on special committees. You realize your boss is on the way up. You've asked for more responsibility and your boss gave you a difficult project to accomplish within a tight

deadline. You've tried a few times to get them to help you with some problems you are having, and they just brush you off. You feel you must be the most incompetent assistant they've ever had.

3. The person who was newly hired to manage your department has never worked in sales before. Their background is in accounting. You can see they're making some very basic mistakes. In a staff meeting, when he/she asks for questions or suggestions, you offer a few helpful hints on how they could improve. Although they try not to show it, you can tell they're irritated. They have ignored you for the past week now, and you don't know what you did wrong.

In the three examples above, the method of communication between boss and employee is not working to either person's advantage. The subordinate may not be able to pinpoint what's wrong, but does sense that the boss is not giving proper guidance to get the job done or that they aren't communicating well.

Example 1. What's going on

In the first example, the boss has encouraged the employee to think of him/her as a 'pal'. There is nothing wrong with a boss having an open-door policy, but when traffic is not controlled and employees rush in with fires to be put out, office gossip or questions they could have easily answered themselves, a manager's precious time vanishes. Likewise, a boss who drops by an employee's cubicle to discuss personal issues while ignoring the project at hand is acting irresponsibly and unprofessionally.

How the boss sees it

The boss can't figure out why her employee is so undermotivated and unable to meet deadlines – why productivity and work quality are poor. After all, the boss gives up precious time to listen to her staff whenever they want to talk.

How the employee sees it

The subordinate finally realizes that they cannot get their work done because of poor supervision and interrupted work habits. When the managerial axe falls, it will be on their head, not their boss's.

What to do

Both boss and employee are wasting each other's time in these cosy chats. The employee should first change his or her behaviour: greatly reduce the amount of time he or she initiates with the boss 'popping into their office' and chatting. If they are interrupted by the boss who begins talking about their personal life, the employee should suggest thcy postpone their conversation until lunch or chat after work. Finally, the employee must discuss any work-related problem they have with the boss as soon as they arise. If it becomes apparent the boss wants to cultivate a friendship, then the employee should suggest they get together outside the office. Friends who work together need to be able to sepa-rate their professional relationship and their friend-ship.

Example 2. What going on

In the second example, the boss is clearly not used to working within an office hierarchy, or at least isn't skilled at managing employees. At first, the picture looked rosy to both the boss and the employee. They're both bright, ambitious people who value a certain degree of autonomy. However, when giving the employee more responsibility, the boss obvious-ly didn't pass along much training or helpful infor-mation.

How the boss sees it

The boss is used to dealing with people who have the experience to complete a project without help. The employee asked for a more interesting project, and the boss gave them one. Now the boss perceives the employee as a nuisance, always pestering with trivial questions. With all the other responsibilities, the boss really doesn't have the time or inclination to nurse this kid along.

How the employee sees it

The deadline is closing in. If the project isn't done right, the employee will look twice as incompetent because he asked for additional work. The relationship with the boss seems to be disintegrating rapidly. The employee really needs help, and doesn't even know how to talk to his boss anymore.

What to do

The employee firsts needs to define clearly the nature of the problem and determine what it will take to solve it. Information? Specialized skills or expertise? Money? Once the problem and the resources needed to complete the project are identified, the employee needs to determine if anyone else can help. If so, he or she can seek help from others. If not, the employee should document the nature of the problem and the solution in a memo to the boss. The key is to communicate concisely. Most bosses hate having to answer a series of unrelated questions or deal with a problem in a piecemeal fashion. Then the subordinate should be assertive about getting a response. If the employee knows the boss is always in the office at 7:30 a.m. or on weekends, he or she should grab a few minutes of the boss's time then. If the employee finds the boss unresponsive, he or she should emphasize the importance of this project, their commitment to it and how they would hate any problems to arise that could prove to be an embarrassment to either of them.

Example 3. What's going on

The employee sees ways to help the new department head be a better manager, but chooses the wrong way to communicate criticism – in a staff meeting. The relationship has been damaged by the employee's tactlessness and the boss's defensiveness.

How the boss sees it

The employee chose the most damaging time to offer suggestions on how to perform better. The boss concludes that either the employee is ignorant of office protocol or is consciously undermining them.

How the employee sees it

The employee believes they were honestly trying to help. Maybe the staff meeting wasn't the best place to offer advice.

What to do

The employee should ask for a few minutes of the boss's time to talk. At that time, the employee should apologize for embarrassing the boss in front of the staff. In addition, the employee should acknowledge a lack of sensitivity and an appreciation for how the boss probably feels. The employee should indicate that even though they got off on the wrong foot, he or she wants to do whatever is possible to support the boss. It is particularly important to understand that these two individuals won't be able to communicate effectively until the air has been cleared regarding the incident.

When communication breaks down, the fragile relationship between boss and employee can be irreparably damaged. The fault is rarely just one person's. As in marriages that falter, both partners in a working relationship contribute their share to the communication problem. If your boss is a good manager, they'll understand their responsibilities and take the initiative to put them into action. When the boss can't or won't attempt to solve a communication problem, however, it's in the employee's best interest to take charge and start looking for solutions.

Communicating directly

One-on-one meetings with bosses are the most direct and focused type of communication. How well you conduct your meeting with your boss depends on how well you prepare.

Here are some guidelines to follow:

1. Organize your thoughts. Know exactly what you want to talk about.

2. Determine what the objective of the meeting is.

3. Determine if your boss is a good candidate for a meeting.

4. Choose the time and place wisely.

Defining your objectives and defining the problem are two different tactics. Before asking for a meeting with your boss, you need to clearly define the problem or issues you want to discuss. If your boss assimilates information better by reading, then prepare an outline or written summary. When you are in the meeting be sure to:

● remain calm and objective;

● describe the objective of your meeting concisely;

● summarize key points that pertain to the topic of discussion;

● present your conclusion, proposed solution or alternative actions that can be taken;

● listen carefully to your boss's response. Does it indicate that they understood what you said? If not, rephrase and summarize to correct any misconceptions;

- when responding to your boss's concerns or objections, restate the specific concern then explain your position;

- seek common ground – points you both agree on;

- seek solutions or an action plan that is mutually acceptable;

- summarize any decisions that are made. Be sure they are understood by both of you.

Consider how you actually speak to your boss. Are you quick to put your thoughts into words – a little too glib – or does it take time to formulate your ideas? Hesitancy on your part can be construed as lack of job knowledge, whereas responding too quickly can make you seem impulsive or abrupt and rude. Practise the following:

1. Time your speech patterns by recording a conversation you might have with your boss. Do you need to slow down or speed up?

2. If you're having trouble verbalizing, give your boss some feedback: 'Bear with me, I'm finding the best way to phrase this....'

3. If you're too quick, give yourself some extra time to respond; count five beats before talking.

Think before you speak and practise putting your thoughts into words. Sometimes we come out of meetings never having said what was really on our minds.

Not all bosses do well in meetings, especially when they're initiated by their employees. Defensive or angry bosses may try all sorts of postponing, stalling and interrupting tactics. Ask yourself the following questions to determine if a meeting with your boss is likely to be productive:

Can your boss take criticism?

A lot of bosses can dish it out but they can't take it. Good bosses, though, want honest feedback from their employees. Realize that there are appropriate times and places to give your boss constructive criticism. The golden rule is never offer your boss criticism in front of others. No matter how well intentioned, it can demoralize and embarrass your boss; it can make you look tactless and blundering.

Is your boss a good problem solver?

No matter how buried in other projects, a good boss will jump right on a problem before it mushrooms into a colossal crisis. Ask yourself the following:

1. Is your boss decisive – not afraid to make a decision, even when it's wrong?

2. Does your boss attack problems or hope they'll go away?

3. Does your boss claim to lack the authority to do anything about it?

Is your boss vindictive?

Does your boss seem open and accepting of what you're saying, then the moment you're out of the office, sharpening the knives? If you're not sure of your boss's character in this regard, ask around. See if there were any co-workers who, after registering complaints or criticism, quit, were fired or transferred to other departments.

Is your boss honest and caring?

An honest boss won't betray what you've said in confidence to hurt others or hurt you. He or she won't use the intimacy of the meeting to lull you into a position of false trust, trying to get you to reveal things you may regret later. If your boss is caring, you'll know it.

Is your boss objective?

Is your boss's self-perception accurate? Can he or she see you in the same light?

One way to encourage a boss's objectivity is to be objective yourself. Your language should never be emotionally laden with phrases like 'You really screwed up when you...'. Try to eliminate all judgemental words from your verbal communication. Words like 'should', 'ought', 'good' and 'bad' only inspire anger and defensiveness in listeners. Always make it clear you're communicating your *observations*, not absolute truth. Avoid sweeping generalizations such as 'Bill *always* makes mistakes'. Stick to the facts. Back up your concerns with evidence.

Is your boss a good listener?

How well does your boss listen? You can tell a lot about listening habits from nonverbal clues:

1. Does your boss make eye contact with you?

2. Does your boss nod in agreement?

3. Does your boss ask thought-provoking questions?

4. Does your boss reiterate main points when you've finished talking?

Or does your boss appear to be intensely uncomfortable, wishing to be anywhere but in the same room with you? A boss who is not listening will:

● try to do two things at once: listen and read a memo, for example;

● play with objects on the desk;

- stare out of the window;

- interrupt frequently.

You might get your boss to be a better listener by suggesting you reschedule the meeting or asking for direct feedback on what you've said, thereby engaging your boss in the discussion.

A meeting with your boss

Following a few simple guidelines will help you achieve what you want from even the most indecisive bosses. You can propose the idea of a meeting to your boss either face to face or in written form, via a memo. Don't ask for a meeting when your boss is:

- visibly upset;

- just out of a difficult meeting with *his/her* boss;

- just arrived in the office;

- about to leave the office;

- in the middle of an important project, preparing for a meeting or presentation, or rushing to meet a deadline.

Tell your boss the purpose of the meeting. Don't keep it a big mystery. While your real objective may be to open up the lines of communication with your boss, this as a reason in itself can sound rather vague and imprecise. Have a tangible purpose and be as specific as possible.

If your boss starts waffling about a convenient time, don't take 'later' for an answer. Keep confronting him or her (politely!) until they agree to a definite date and time.

How to prepare

If your purpose is to define mutual expectations, write a memo to give your boss before the meeting, detailing the problems you'd like clarification on. Be specific. Avoid generalizations. Cite particular instances and dates: inability to get shipments to customers on time, problems in putting together sales reports, need for funding on a special project.

Remember, your boss doesn't have a lot of time to spend reading pages of intricately worded prose. If you've presented your boss with a 20-page memo *before* the meeting, they may lose all interest in accommodating your requests, foreseeing the mountains of paperwork you'll generate. Stick to the facts. Don't exaggerate. And keep an objective, non-accusatory tone.

How to conduct a meeting

During any introductory small talk and throughout the meeting, be aware of the body language each of you projects. It can tell you a lot more than the actual words the person is speaking.

Check for openness and genuine interest. Remember, this applies as much to you as to your boss. If you find yourself slouching in the chair, arms folded, turning away – sit up straight, place your feet on the floor and assume an attentive, responsive expression – no matter how defensive your boss's words make you feel.

Watch for body language with a positive meaning:

- open, relaxed position, facing each other squarely;

- arms at sides or hands folded casually in lap;

- good eye contact;

- pleasant, attentive facial expression;

- good posture.

If your boss exhibits some or all of these traits, it means you're coming through loud and clear, and he or she is receiving the information in a positive manner.

You should also watch for body language with a more negative interpretation:

- crossed arms;

- body in a sideways position;

- frowning or stone-faced expression;
- frequently looking at watch;
- tapping toe;
- drumming fingers.

If you see any of these traits, stop – unless your objective is to make your boss even more uncomfortable. One effective way of reducing negative body language is to engage your boss directly in the exchange of information. You can ask for feedback by saying, 'How do you feel about some of these problems I've touched on?' This way you can address any misunderstandings immediately.

Even when it's your boss's turn to do the talking, you still have to be watchful and aware – not only of what your boss is saying, but the kind of information you're giving nonverbally.

In stressful situations which carry an emotional impact – such as meetings with our bosses – it's tempting to stop paying attention when the other party is speaking and think of what you're going to say next. By not 'tracking' we lose part of what the other person is saying. It's easy for them to 'read' our impatience to speak. Be sure when your boss is talking that you give constant feedback, both verbal and nonverbal by:

- attending – assume straight posture, make eye contact, nod in agreement when appropriate;

- asking thought-provoking questions when he pauses for feedback;

- encouraging him by saying, 'I'm really interested in hearing your reaction to this....';

- reiterating what your boss has said to show you understand.

Asking thought-provoking questions may sound difficult, especially when you're already nervous about presenting your end of the discussion persuasively. But if you learn to listen closely, you'll pick up on key points. Asking for further illumination will not displease your boss. In fact, he or she will be impressed with your ability to quickly grasp the points of discussion.

Repeating what your boss said allows you to paraphrase his or her argument. You can begin by summarizing essential points: 'You're saying that, first, we should eliminate undue spending within the department to increase production figures by next quarter. Second, that our re-staffing needs will have to wait.'

Ending a meeting

A meeting usually ends with the two parties reaching a mutual agreement. When it's you and your boss it's usually a performance agreement that satisfies the needs of both parties. Your meeting purpose and performance agreement could look like this:

Purpose of meeting
For my boss to be more specific about what kind of informational feedback he/she needs from me and at what times.

Performance agreement
My boss and I agree to meet once a week to discuss the written reports I turn in to him/her outlining the duties, accomplishments and status of my staff. At the end of each month we will review goals for the next month.

Remember to make your performance agreement as specific and concise as possible. No one likes to leave a meeting with a performance agreement which is too imprecise for performance to be measured against. For instance, stay away from generalities like 'schedule more meetings with boss'.

When it's time for you to shake hands and come out of the office smiling, make sure you end the meeting in a spirit of co-operation. Thank your boss for his/her time. They have done you a favour, even if it's going to work to their benefit, too.

How to follow up a meeting

After your meeting, write your boss a memo detailing the important points and the decisions that were reached. You might want to include a phrase like, 'If this is not your understanding of what transpired, please let me know'. That way, should there be any future discussion of you not keeping up your end of the performance agreement, you have *your* understanding of the meeting's results in writing.

Arrange for a follow-up meeting in the near future to see how both you and your boss are dealing with the changes you've introduced. Remember, improving your communication with your boss doesn't come from a single meeting, but from a series of fine tunings and adjustments until you have a system that works for both of you.

How to communicate in writing

As we mentioned earlier, all written communication – memos, reports, notes – should be concise, well organized and well thought out.

Remember the cardinal rules of memo writing:

1. Never communicate through memos when you're angry.

2. Never communicate through memos information you wouldn't want others to see.

Even when you write a memo that's 'confidential and private' it doesn't guarantee that an unscrupulous boss won't use the information to further himself or to hurt you.

Realize that any time you write for business purposes, it's like advertising your own mental processes. This can either work for you or against you. Make sure:

- content is well organized and structured correctly;

- ideas are communicated clearly;

- memos contain no grammar, spelling or punctuation errors.

Even though you may be able to blame clerical errors on your secretary, you're still ultimately responsible for anything that goes out with your name on it. Use memos and reports to communicate to others – including your boss – what a professional you are.

Summary

In this chapter we've talked about how to build better communication with your boss through a series of steps:

1. Determine if you and your boss are having communication problems. Keep in mind that both boss and subordinate usually contribute to the problem. Assess the behaviour and work habits of both you and your boss.

2. Decide if a one-on-one meeting with your boss is the most effective way to solve your communication problem. Determine whether your boss is a good candidate for a

meeting. Prepare by clearly identifying your purpose, the projected outcome and what you want to communicate.

3. To set up a meeting with your boss, you need to ask them at an appropriate time, and prepare a pre-meeting memo outlining what you plan to cover and the communication problems you're having.

4. During the meeting, pay attention to the nonverbal feedback you're getting from and giving to your boss. Stay focused and responsive.

5. After the meeting, be sure to thank your boss for his/her time. Follow up with any necessary documentation: summary memos or performance agreements.

8

Bad bosses: what they can do to you and how you can stop them

Probably everyone, at one time or another, has worked for a bad boss. In some cases, how bad your boss is can be measured by how much he or she squelches your own career. If you have networked effectively within your company and have friends in high places, you might be able to tolerate your bad boss until you can transfer to a good boss. If, however, your boss is involved in unethical behaviour or sexual harassment, you really can't afford to continue working for them.

In this chapter we'll look at some characteristics of bad, even intolerable bosses. We'll also talk about how they can hinder you by:

- blocking your career moves;
- taking credit for your achievements;
- undermining your credibility.

Then we'll look at some effective strategies you can adopt to deal with these individuals.

The bad bosses – who are they?

A recent survey of good and bad bosses showed that even good bosses are usually tainted with some bad habits or behaviours. It's not unusual for inspiring, charismatic bosses to display a certain amount of egotism, or for technical geniuses to be a little aloof towards their staff. It all comes with the territory.

Ask yourself the following questions:

1. Does your boss consistently avoid promoting people from this department into positions of higher authority?

2. Have any charges of sexual harassment ever been brought against your boss?

3. Is there a high turnover of personnel in the department?

4. Does your boss talk disparagingly about people behind their backs?

5. Does your boss use his anger to intimidate subordinates, peers, superiors?

6. Is your boss competitive in conversation, having to be constantly one-up on others?

7. Does your boss steal credit from subordinates for projects they complete?

8. Do talented employees threaten your boss?

If you answered 'yes' to any one of the above questions, it's likely you're stuck with a bad boss. Let's take a closer look at some specific types and how they operate.

Incompetent bosses

If you work for a boss who's incompetent, chances are they have still got their job because *their* boss knows they're no threat and wants your boss exactly where they are. Incompetent bosses like to delay any kind of decisions as long as possible. They hate to demonstrate strong leadership and think only in terms of avoidance rather than creative solutions. Innovation is the bane of their existence; so is conflict. They avoid hiring and firing employees, performance reviews, soliciting employee feedback and meeting project deadlines.

To mask their incompetence, this kind of boss will form committees, set up fact-finding studies and hire outside consultants. But the real problems never get resolved because incompetent bosses neither listen nor learn.

Often incompetent bosses have been promoted

from areas within the company where they had some real technical expertise. They might have been more comfortable working as 'independent contributors' than as team leaders; thus they tend to panic when management skills are required.

They also might be where they are because of who they know. You'll recognize incompetent bosses by their:

- avoidance of conflict at any cost;

- tendency to interrupt others, drone on, not listen, avoid eye contact;

- fear of more capable employees who might take their jobs or expose their inadequacies;

- inability to grasp the essentials required for acceptable job performance.

If you think you're working for an incompetent boss, compare notes with co-workers. How do they react to his supervision? Look for facts, not opinions or gossip. Find out, if you can, what your boss's track record is with your company and with former companies where they have worked. Does your boss change jobs a lot? Complain of having been mistreated and unfairly dealt with? If so, it's likely that other companies realized your boss's incompetence and took action.

Try to determine how soon, if at all, your incompetent boss will be led to the company's chopping-block. Ask yourself:

- Will administration eventually wake up and do something about my boss's chronic mis-management?

- Is it possible or appropriate for me to make my boss's inadequacies known?

- What is my track record with this company?

- Can I risk being labelled a complainer by upper management?

- Can my career afford having this person as my manager?

Executives often look bad if they promote or protect incompetent bosses. However, it might not be to your advantage to complain about your incompetent boss. Therefore, you may have to work with your incompetent boss – support and organize and do their job.

By carefully documenting your work for your incompetent boss you may be able to get yourself promoted and transferred into another department – something your present boss would never dream of doing for you.

Powerholics

The only issue powerholic bosses care about is if they're in the driver's seat. Working for powerholics can be a tough assignment. You've got to walk a fine line between being competent enough to make them

look good yet not challenging them with your in-
dependence or ability.

The key word for powerholics is *control*. They've
got to control everyone and everything around
them, no matter how insignificant their place on the
corporate pyramid.

Here are some characteristics of powerholics:

● They rarely provide subordinates with a
chance to advance.

● They don't delegate well, claiming subordinates do such a poor job, 'I just have to do it
over again myself'.

● They're single-minded and egomaniacal,
sacrificing the good of the company for the
growth of their own little empires.

● They're not receptive to innovation, particularly when *their* ways of doing things are
challenged.

● They're often overbearing, demanding, con-
temptuous and bullying.

When devising strategies to use when working
with a powerholic boss, try determining:

1. How much power does my boss *really* have?
Does it reside completely in the position or
do they possess some personal power as
well?

2. How vital is my department within the corporate power flow? What essential services does it perform?

3. What kind of power does my boss have with their immediate boss? A lot? Or none?

4. Can I make a successful lateral move to another department without damaging my present position?

In other words, determine if your boss's power is real or imagined. Companies often give these individuals departments to control that have no real effect on bottom-line profit and loss margins. If your boss is merely a paper tiger, try to find out if there's a boss elsewhere in your company with some real power, influence and heart. Then make it clear you'd like to transfer to that department where you'd be given more responsibility. If your boss really does have power, find out if they're willing to give subordinates a hand-up by becoming a mentor. This approach may appeal sufficiently to their ego that they will help you. Whatever the outcome, look for ways you can learn from the experience – whether it is job skills you're learning or improved interpersonal management skills.

Indifferent bosses

You'll know you're working for an indifferent boss when the workplace feels like a mortuary.

Indifferent bosses cast a cloud of listlessness that is difficult for even the most eager subordinates to overcome. Perhaps their indifference stems from a woefully botched job of corporate miscasting. Rather than heading a marketing department they'd rather be trying out that new lens on their camera. In any case, their apathy shows; and unless you're careful, you could end up being just like your boss: indifferent.

Ask yourself the following questions to determine the extent of your boss's indifference:

1. Does your boss use the bureaucracy as an excuse for not doing anything: 'I'd really like to help you, but the rules and regulations state...'?

2. Is your boss burned-out from too many years on the fast track?

3. Is your boss experiencing too many conflicting priorities: career, family, health and money?

4. Is your boss cynical; does he or she discourage any attempts at team building?

5. Does your boss discourage feedback?

Nothing is more deflating than being stuck with an indifferent boss. They usually hold on to their position through seniority or some quirk of expertise. If you complain about their attitude to co-workers they might sympathize: 'But he's got to stay in charge of operations because he's the only guy who can get this computer system back on line.'

If your boss is burned out from too much job-related travel, family pressures or spending nearly every weekend at the office, encourage him or her to open up and look at some options. Here are a few suggestions that may help:

- a morale-building weekend retreat for the whole department;
- motivational seminars;
- weekly staff meetings to encourage feedback.

Remember, your boss's lack of caring permeates the entire department. Perhaps hiding beneath a shell of indifference is your boss's way of protecting their job from ambitious subordinates. Ask yourself:

1. Is your boss really indifferent, depressed and uncaring or is this some kind of defensive strategy?

2. Does your boss's behaviour continue at home/in the community or does it change when he or she leaves the office?

3. How does working for your boss affect your pride in your work?

4. Do other bosses in the company value your boss's work?

5. Is your boss merely a poor leader?

6. Can you find something about their perfor-
    mance that is outstanding and compliment
    them on that?

7. Is your boss threatened by motivated
    employees?

8. Does your boss suffer from low self-esteem?

Many employees find that the greatest joy comes
not just from performing their jobs well, but from
camaraderie that results from teamwork. When
your boss denies you these benefits, it's difficult to
keep the quality of your work high. In this case, you
must evaluate how much longer you can afford to
work for such a boss without your own attitude slipping. If your boss is capable of change – that is, if
their attitude is the result of a specific incident and
not habitual – do you want to get involved in helping them recover? Assess how much energy you
have, whether you can help rehabilitate your boss or
whether you need to seek outside professional help.

Neurotic bosses

Nothing can make your job harder than working for
a boss whose management style is impaired by their
inability to control emotions. This usually surfaces
in a neurotic pattern of behaviour that, depending
on your boss's position on the corporate ladder, can
affect the tone of the whole company.

Neurotic bosses have a million ways of keeping you in your place or helping you out of the door. The last place they want to see you move is above them, beside them or working for another boss in the same company. They're afraid you're going to spill the beans about how incompetent, lazy, cynical and emotionally out of kilter they are. Besides, who knows better than you about their secret rages, their unfair performance reviews, their squandering of company time and money through poor planning?

Good employees jeopardize a neurotic boss's security. Here are some ways to recognize a neurotic boss's style and what you can do about it.

Tough, angry bosses

You can be thankful that, as a trend, the 'tough angry management style' is almost over. But as a personality trait, a lot of bosses still believe it's all right to brutalize their employees in an effort to force peak performance out of them.

If you've got a tough, angry boss, time is on your side. Changing attitudes in the 1990s have forced managers to put more emphasis on valuing employees rather than browbeating them. Yet, the planned obsolescence of the tough, angry boss doesn't make your job any easier – especially when that boss overworks, underpays and publicly berates employees.

What they can do to you

Tough bosses are usually valued by those above them, while those below them suffer. They manage to get the job done and to meet bottom-line requirements. Your tough boss may have support, even full approval, from upper management. Therefore, they're in an ideal position to do some real damage to their employees by discrediting them.

- *Undermine your credibility.* As far as the company is concerned, your only window on the world is through your boss. A boss who doesn't like you or is secretly afraid of you can tarnish your record, deny your contribution and do their utmost to make sure no other boss in the company will welcome you into their department.

- *Block your career moves.* The annual performance review is where it all happens. This is the big showdown between boss and employee, where – after a year of hard work – you can walk away with more money and a promotion or absolutely nothing. Watch for these favourite ploys of a tough, angry boss during your annual review:

  - *The accusatory review.* Tough, angry bosses do not like to reward employees – even hard-working ones. They derive power from throwing others off balance and keeping them guessing. Rather than recognizing your achievements and contributions, your tough boss will berate you with your failures and shortcomings. Money is another big control issue with them, so they'll probably give you as little as possible.

What you can do

Tough, angry bosses are essentially bullies who enjoy intimidating employees. Their arrogance, however, does create a few blind spots. Your boss probably overestimates his or her control not only over their employees but with lateral bosses as well.

You need the chance to prove your worth to someone other than this tyrant. Look around. Surely not every boss in your company believes that your boss is so wonderful. Some are probably as secretly nauseated by his/her arrogance, unfairness and intimidation as you are.

See if there is a neutral party you can talk to: a company ombudsman, an employee assistance programme. Make sure your job performance is good; keep records of your accomplishments, attendance and productivity. When the opportunity arises, seek a transfer within the company – to a better boss.

Finally, stand up to your boss in an appropriate, self-confident manner when he or she is abusive or tries to intimidate you. If your boss makes accusations, insist that they back up their comments with facts. If your boss tries to intimidate you through implied or direct threats regarding your job security, tell them your work record will speak for itself and you'll be happy to discuss the matter before a review board or a mediating organization for unfair employment practices.

You can short-circuit the effects of the accusatory review by going into the meeting prepared with documentation of your achievements. Try to ensure that another boss is present. Bullies don't like to go public unless they're sure of their support. If your boss is allowed to prevail and you know he or she is being deliberately unfair, don't try to confront them. A tough, angry boss thrives on personal conflict and verbal abuse. You'll only come out bruised and battered. Several courses of action are open to you. One is to go to your boss's boss. Another is to file a grievance.

When you go over your boss's head you've declared war, so be prepared for a vindictive response. Various schools of thought exist about when it's appropriate to go over your boss's head. They are:

1. *Never*. It violates the chain of command. Other bosses view it as insubordination.

2. *Sometimes*. But only go to lateral bosses, never to your boss's boss.

3. *Situational*. When you have no alternative, go to your boss's boss.

If you're going to complain to a higher authority, make sure you do it properly: make an appointment beforehand and have proper documentation. If possible, have tape recordings or notes in your boss's handwriting to refute any possible charges that you've manufactured the evidence against your boss.

The purpose of going to your boss's boss or to a boss in another department is to hold your boss accountable, since he or she feels no need for accountability to employees.

If your boss's boss does not resolve the situation to your satisfaction, you're entitled to complain to your personnel department. This procedure varies from company to company.

It sounds as though it should work, but it often doesn't. Because of the office grapevine, the subject of grievance procedures, which should remain confidential, often doesn't. Depending on the amount of power they wield, bad bosses can escape unscathed, while the employees suffer the consequences of going back to work for the tough, angry boss they've ratted on.

You can also file grievance procedures outside the company which are handled through laws regarding equal opportunity and unfair work practices.

Paternalistic/maternalistic bosses

Some bosses are most comfortable reliving patterns they learned as children, interacting with their mother and father. It seems logical to them, now that they're adults with responsibility for employees, that they assume the role of a parent.

There's the boss who views subordinates as a 'family' and thinks of himself as the stern but loving father, who 'mothers' employees, encouraging them to confide all their problems. These paternalistic/ maternalistic bosses may be well intentioned, but they've overlooked the glaring fact that the office is not the home. Their behaviour is unprofessional and unflattering to boss and employee alike.

Paternalistic male bosses, especially, are not comfortable assigning women stereotypical roles. They view female employees not only as daughters but also as wives and mothers. A woman's place, they believe, is in the home – preferably in the kitchen, nursery, laundry or bedroom. Female subordinates may find that paternalistic bosses refuse to take them seriously, preferring instead to patronize them. Similarly, male employees may have trouble deflecting numerous queries and advice about their private life from maternalistic bosses.

If you're in this situation, ask yourself the following questions:

1. What does my boss get out of acting like everybody's mother/father?

2. What issues does my boss manage to avoid by interacting with subordinates in this manner?

3. How do I threaten my boss when I don't act like a daughter/son? Like a dutiful wife? Like a devoted parent?

It could be that your paternalistic/maternalistic boss is trying to hang on to power by building a sense of loyalty through guilt. A boss often adopts this kind of behaviour to mask a lack of expertise or competence. Be careful how you respond. Choose your remarks carefully. When confronted, a paternalistic/maternalistic boss can drop the parental act and turn mean and nasty.

What they can do to you

Basically, the worst thing a paternalistic/maternalistic boss can do to you is through power of association. Other bosses and co-workers in your company may think that you're just as unprofessional and ineffectual as your boss.

The paternalistic/maternalistic boss is often displaying a kind of passive/aggressive behaviour. Unlike an angry boss, this kind of boss doesn't readily acknowledge their anger. They excel at making *you* angry, however. And if you react negatively to their patronizing, snooping or cloying behaviour, they'll merely respond with hurt bewilderment.

If you do too good a job working for mother or father, they may be unwilling to promote you. Your department is just 'one big happy family' as far as they're concerned and you've found your place.

Convincing your paternalistic/maternalistic boss that you deserve more – whether it's a raise, a promotion or just plain professional treatment – can be difficult. They're not especially good at listening.

What you can do

When you meet with your boss, be sure to follow some basic guidelines:

1. Know what you want. Be specific.

2. Stay on the subject; reiterate your goals when the conversation goes off course.

3. Be professional. Don't make jokes, small talk or spend a lot of time listening to your boss's anecdotes. Your boss might see this as hostile behaviour, but it's life in the real world – the world of business.

4. If your boss starts waffling, provide closure and structure. 'A week from Thursday, then, I'm to have the improved sales figures for all my accounts to you for review?'

Competitive bosses

Bosses compete with employees in all sorts of ways, both overtly and covertly. Men traditionally compete with each other, both as bosses of younger male employees and with their executive peers. Male employees are often plunged into fierce competition by top-performing female co-workers and bosses.

If you're a woman with a female boss, a certain amount of friction already exists. In a recent study, 47 per cent of the women polled said they would prefer to work for a man, and 30–44 per cent of the men polled said their boss's gender made no difference.

It's an acknowledged law of the workplace that women compete against women more fiercely and for far fewer rewards than men compete against men. If you're female and you have a competitive female boss, you might want to ask yourself the following questions:

1. What is it that we compete for most strongly? Money, men, attention, expertise?

2. What does she have to gain from making her employees look bad?

3. How do other bosses see me? Is she hurting my career, or do they expect me to deal with her and move on?

Even when you're a male employee of a competitive female boss, you're not exempt from her furious drive to prove herself. She may even see you as more of a threat than female employees because, as a man, she believes you're more promotable – into her position. Both men and women bosses can be competitive. And both can be equally hard to deal with. The best approach to dealing with a competitive boss is to find ways to promote teamwork with your boss and create a relationship built on trust rather than competition.

What they can do to you

Competitive bosses take credit for your achievements. Unless your achievements are documented and on file, your boss may try stealing your ideas and then stealing your credit and promotion. Competitive, unscrupulous bosses look for talented, inexperienced employees who will mistake their boss's sharpened interest in their new management strategy or a sales incentive as true appreciation.

What you can do

Employees will probably have to let the incident pass the first time it happens. If it looks as though your boss is developing a pattern of taking credit for your achievements, you can:

1. Document to others your participation in projects, particularly to other bosses or your boss's boss if possible. Do this through: reports and memos written by you; active participation in meetings; working late/ coming in early to work on a project and making sure other bosses see you and know what you're working on; suggesting an

article be written in the employee newsletter (if appropriate) on your project; and saving any memos or correspondence that may support and document your role.

2. Push for visibility and recognition elsewhere. Realize that you may never get your boss to acknowledge your participation.

3. Meet with your boss privately when he or she blatantly refuses to recognize your involvement (not listing your name as the author of a report or participant in a project). Call the omission to their attention calmly and objectively. Ask for the error to be corrected.

Deviant bosses

Deviant bosses look like everybody else. You can only spot them by working with them. And all too often, your career can't afford the damage they cause. If you suspect your boss of deviant behaviour, it's essential you line up hard facts to support your allegations. Rumours circulated by co-workers don't count. Document your facts, talk to upper management and if nothing changes, get away from your boss. As fast as you can. The following are two different types of deviant bosses.

The drug or alcohol abuser

Twenty years ago two or three drinks at lunchtime

were part of a powerful boss's minimal daily requirement, just as low cholesterol diets are today. Times have changed and so has the public's awareness of the damage alcohol can cause to physical and emotional well-being. Alcohol abuse is easier to detect than drug abuse. If you see that your boss is openly abusing alcohol, chances are his productivity at work is slipping. Doubtless, their family life is in turmoil, too. Here are some warning signs:

● coming to work late, taking late lunches;

● low energy level;

● shoddy work performance, little follow-through;

● abusive behaviour;

● bouts of depression, low self-esteem;

● financial problems.

The symptoms of drug abuse are similar to alcohol abuse, yet drugs are deemed much less socially acceptable. For one thing, unless they're prescribed by a physician, they're illegal. Some upper-level managers have found themselves unwittingly trapped in a cycle of drug dependency that began as an effort to numb the stress they encountered in their jobs.

What you can do

Find out who is the best, most receptive person to discuss this problem with. It may be a personnel manager, an employee ombudsman or your boss's boss. Regardless, have your facts clearly document-ed. Present the information with compassion for your boss and from the standpoint that you're doing what's best for your boss and the company. Finally, ask for confidentiality. If your supporting evidence is convincing, there's no reason for you to become involved any further.

The sexual harasser

It's not unusual for conflicts to arise when men work for women, or women work for men, in the modern world of business. Although these conflicts may be job related, they usually stem from underlying sex-ual tension.

Women bosses can sexually harass male employ-ees, but the occurrences of such behaviour are rare compared to the reverse: male bosses making female employees feel that granting them sexual favours is all part of the job.

If you're a woman and are wondering if your boss's growing attentiveness is out of bounds, ask yourself:

1. Does my boss compliment me or stare unnecessarily when I wear clothing that's more 'feminine'?

2. Does he 'accidentally' touch parts of my body?

3. Does he stop when I ask him to?

4. Does he pester me by calling me at home?

5. Does he threaten me when I warn him I'm going to file a complaint?

6. Does he treat all women like an office harem?

7. Is turnover high among females in his department?

8. Does he ask me to stay late and work with him when the project isn't crucial?

9. Have charges of sexual harassment ever been brought against him?

Sexual harassment doesn't have to culminate in sex. It also includes any kind of innuendo, teasing, attention to one's dress, 'accidental' fondling or pestering that the employee finds unwelcome and inappropriate. Bosses accused of sexual harassment often respond that the employee dressed in a provocative manner or was openly flirtatious. Therefore, it's imperative your dress and demeanour – even when 'playing around' – be completely professional and above board. Be prepared for lack of co-operation or denial when you ask your boss to stop. He may consider it all part of the game, that women say 'no' when they really mean 'yes'.

And if you go above his head, to *his* boss, or register a formal complaint, be prepared for possible reper cussions.

Some companies don't like employees who rock the boat – that includes standing up to a boss who sexually harasses female employees. Even if you have to leave the company to escape this situation, you'll know that by taking formal action against him – unlike others who silently and swiftly disappeared before – your complaint constitutes the beginning of a record against which your boss's subsequent behaviour can be measured.

What a sexually harassing boss can do to you

Your deviant boss might use angry outbursts or physical threats to quell any thought of exposing his sexual harassment to higher authorities. He might use subtler methods of intimidation: threatening dismissal or tarnishing your reputation – letting it be known any attempt at seduction originated with you.

What you can do

If he seems unbalanced enough to carry out his threats or act on his anger, you should make your fears known to those who can restrain him. Document and, if possible, tape record his outbursts, threats or innuendos, then take your case to the big bosses.

Public strategies to stop bad bosses

Confronting a boss is never easy. Confronting a bad boss is a lot harder because you have a pretty good idea, before you even start, how things will end. Most executives won't even listen to your complaints about your bad boss unless you have documented your complaint and confronted him or her first.

When an employee fails to stop a boss's serious wrongdoing by working within the company structure, they may choose to go public. Never go public without hard evidence which supports your complaint. The following are some strategies for going public:

1. *Whistle blowing.* Whistle blowing means turning your boss in to the media, government agencies or law enforcement officials. Employees who go to this length must be prepared to pay the price of a long and public fight. They're usually not employed by the company they decide to blow the whistle on. Sometimes they're reinstated in their old jobs, but they're stuck with the stigma of being disloyal, demented, even dangerous

   When whistle blowers are still employed by their companies it is illegal for employers to retaliate.

2. *Legal action.* Employees who lose their jobs

and thirst not only for vindication but also justice can take legal action against their former employers, thanks to legislation passed during the last 20 years. If you're planning to take legal action, find out about your rights as an employee in respect of discrimination, harassment or unfair dismissal.

Summary

In this chapter we've looked at various types of bad bosses, how they can make you look bad and can have a negative impact on your career.

Remember these guidelines when taking action against them:

1. Regardless of the approach you choose, always be able to back up your allegation with facts.

2. Taking assertive action against a bad boss begins by direct one-on-one confrontation. Spell out what you don't like, how you want to see things change.

3. If that doesn't work, try going over your boss's head, talking to *his or her* boss.

4. If that doesn't work, try filing a grievance.

5. Public strategies include:

- whistle-blowing;
- legal action.

9

Good bosses: what they can do for you and how you can manage them

If you're working for a good boss, you already know it. Tolstoy once wrote that 'Happy families resemble one another, each unhappy family is unhappy in its own way'. While not all good bosses are the same kind of people, their effect on their employees can be summed up in a few key phrases. Good bosses:

- help you get where you want to go;

- take time to listen;

- delegate, make full use of their staff's resources;

- take chances;

- make coming to work fun;

- add a sense of purpose and excitement to even the most mundane assignments;

- build loyal teams;

- are strong leaders, good role models.

In this chapter we'll look at three kinds of good bosses:

1.   team builders;

2.   motivators and delegators;

3.   charismatic leaders.

We'll also examine what good bosses can do for you, what you can learn from them, and how you can manage a good boss.

Why should you take the time to understand your good boss? Because you can learn valuable lessons about managing, team building and sustaining positive work relationships. These lessons will help you in the future if you become the 'boss'.

Not all good bosses share the same strengths. It's important to know what makes your boss so great. Is it their willingness to stick up for their employees, their honesty and sense of fair play, or their sense of humour? Try making a list of your boss's ten most valuable characteristics, then prioritize them according to which mean the most to you. Your list might look something like this:

- strength;

- helpfulness;

- sense of humour;

- inspiration;

- good manager;

- understanding;

- good team builder;

- creativity;

- decisiveness;

- kindness.

Team builders

Probably the best qualification your boss can have for being truly outstanding is his ability to build a strong, loyal team. If your boss is a good *team-builder*, his abilities include:

- perceives and fully uses the strengths of each team member;

- inspires loyalty on behalf of team members by his accountability;

- encourages co-operation among team members by emphasizing fair play;

- can be a hero (every team needs one).

Good team builders, like good coaches, want players with differing abilities to play specific positions. They know the inherent value in diversity – the more diverse a culture, the greater its strength. Therefore, they don't expect all team members to be alike or play alike. A good manager will take the time to listen to his staff members, get to know each one and learn what motivates each one individually and as part of a team.

What team builders can do for you

By working for a good team builder you'll learn how to play as part of a team to accomplish a common goal. By becoming part of the process, you become invested in the outcome. The team's goals become your goals.

When introducing a new project, a good team builder helps you:

- understand the importance of the project;

- appreciate how your involvement is critical and how you will benefit from the project's success;

- find your own work rhythm.

Most important, you can learn how individual contributions can be incorporated and transformed into an all-consuming group effort. A boss that is a good coach can get his or her team to play together by building trust. With trust, groups can gather and process data more quickly, and respond to change with greater flexibility.

As a team member, you may also experience more open conflict with team members and with your boss. Yet conflict, based on trust, is honest and healthy. If your boss has built a strong team, it can lead to greater creativity and awareness.

How you can manage your team-building boss

As much as your boss may emphasize the equal status of all team members (including himself), each team also needs a leader – someone they can respect, respond to. To be an effective coach, your boss needs feedback. The more your boss has fostered an atmosphere of trust, the more honest feedback you can give them.

1. Let your boss know your feelings and opinions, even when they conflict with his or hers.

2. Let your boss know if he/she is dictating their wishes to the team rather than listening.

3. Let your boss know if he or she represented your team fairly to upper-level management.

4. Don't take your boss's criticisms personally.

5. Communicate your appreciation when your boss rewards the team for achieving a mutually defined goal.

Motivators and delegators

Good bosses, just like good parents, thrive on knowing they've helped employees grow from employeehood into becoming good bosses themselves. Two ways in which they can nurture development in promising employees is through motivating and delegating.

It's no surprise that bosses who motivate others well are good at communicating their interest in their subordinates. Some companies try motivating employees through incentive programmes, bonuses and increased perks. While these financial stimulants may produce short-term improvement in job performance, they can leave employees feeling like burned-out machines whose only function is to work faster and harder.

Employees want bosses who care, who take a sincere interest in them, their families, their lives.

What motivators can do for you

To truly motivate you, a good boss must also help you develop your talent, use your creativity and push you where you want to go. To do this, a motivating boss can either offer to become your mentor or help you network.

Mentoring, or providing 'help from above', is a powerful motivator to succeed. It's one way good bosses can show they care about promising employees by lending a helping hand. Mentoring can range from giving detailed guidance and advice to general encouragement. It's a wide-ranging show of support given from a person in a powerful position to an employee over a period of time.

A mentor doesn't have to be one's immediate boss. Mentors are sometimes bosses in other departments, or experts in one's chosen field. They can act as good role models, advocates or instructors. Sometimes an employee chooses a mentor, or sometimes a mentor volunteers advice to an employee. In a few situations the relationship is institutionalized – companies have instituted a formalized structure where aspiring employees can go for executive help. Mentors can move you upwards in the corporate organization by:

- acting as your sponsor;

- recommending you to bigger bosses;

- including you in special projects that help you see how the business world works.

A mentor can show you the ropes, cut through corporate red tape and introduce you to sources it

would ordinarily take you years to find and cultivate. Mentoring is also a way for a boss to groom his
replacement.

If, for some reason, your boss can't help you
upwards, sometimes he or she can help you move
laterally into other bosses' departments or outwards
into other organizations. This kind of support is
called networking.

A good boss who is networking for you is basically selling another potential boss your abilities. Your
boss will be using the following selling tools:

- your proven track record;
- evidence of untapped abilities that would be
  better used in another department or company;
- knowledge of your overall goals and career
  plans;
- wanting what's best for you.

Networking takes place not only in the immediate
workplace, but also in social settings, within professional organizations and among friends. A good
boss recognizes the importance of these connections
and uses them to help promising employees get
where they want to go.

How you can manage a motivating boss

The best way to manage a boss who is a good motivator is to succeed. Live the lessons they're teaching you and show them you're an eager and willing student. Don't disappoint them through unprofessional behaviour or laziness caused by thinking you've got it made now that they are helping you.

Motivators thrive on enthusiasm, encouragement and feedback. You, in turn, can motivate *your* boss by:

- performing well;

- showing a respectful interest in your boss and their life outside the office;

- learning all you can from them;

- teaching him/her – giving them the value of your expertise.

- sharing with them your innovative thinking, your creative solutions.

Use your boss. That's what he/she is there for. Use them as a role model, a mentor, even as a competitor if that keeps you motivated. The more you show you want to learn, the more they'll teach you.

Bosses who delegate

As companies grow, bosses get busier. Good bosses quickly learn the value in delegating responsibility to subordinates – before their departments feel the effects of their myriad commitments. Some bosses have to be pressured into delegating, others seize on the opportunity. The beauty of good delegation is that it accomplishes several goals simultaneously.

What a delegating boss can do for you

A boss who delegates well delegates fairly, giving all team members a shot at assignments that can increase their share in the spoils. Delegation also fosters a team's confidence in its leader to prioritize: knowing which projects are crucial, which can be handed around, which call for immediate action.

Your delegating boss can:

- show you they think you're good enough to be trusted with important responsibility;

- give you a chance to prove yourself on a new project;

- take full advantage of your talents;

- groom you for promotion by increasing your visibility to upper-level management.

Once again, delegation is an effective means for a manager to build trust and greater team spirit among subordinates. It shows that the boss trusts those who work for him/her, causing subordinates to produce more, offer honest feedback and develop into more highly skilled employees.

How you can manage your delegating boss

Your delegating boss has shown confidence that you can do a new job, take on a new project. His or her trust is both stimulating and stress producing. It's a test you don't want to fail, yet perhaps you lack information or expertise to perform with confidence.

Keep the lines of communication open. Your boss has delegated to you not only because he or she is busy but because they know you're ready. Don't hesitate to:

- ask plenty of questions, get information;

- give your boss feedback on your approach;

- pass the stress test of learning something new; remain professional and competent;

- show you're trustworthy;

- meet deadlines;

- accept your boss's criticism;

- volunteer for extra assignments.

Charismatic leaders

People love a winner. They like voting for winning presidents, betting on winning horses, playing on winning teams. That's because winning is infectious. People like being around highly charismatic leaders because some of their positive energy rubs off.

A charismatic leader can accomplish one very important goal much more easily than other kinds of leaders: obliterating differences and integrating opposing forces into one powerful group.

What a charismatic boss can do for you

Perform well and your charismatic boss can do a lot for you. Perhaps he or she sees possibilities in you that far exceed his or her own accomplishments. Your boss can tell you what pitfalls to avoid, what seeming shortcuts will only derail your career. See if your charismatic boss interacts with you in any of the following ways. Does your boss:

- inspire self-confidence in you;

- make a dull job fun;

- communicate a sense of mission;

- make you proud to be on the team;

- value and understand your contributions and increase your visibility – not only within the company, but within the community as well?

To work effectively with his or her team, a charismatic leader must be accessible to team members, otherwise motivation can quickly fade.

How you can manage a charismatic boss

Charismatic leaders, just like their less dramatic fellow managers, have to be team players, not just team owners. To be effective, they must also be able to demonstrate they can plan a crusade as well as lead one.

It's not unusual for highly charismatic people to be rather ineffective at detailed work, organizing and intensive planning. Find out where your boss's weaknesses lie, then give badly-needed support.

With a charismatic boss, you can:

- take charge; be self-motivating – this boss is not interested in supervising daily routines;

- master the details of running the office;

- make him or her look good, giving support where they need it and keeping their public image intact;

- give feedback. They need to know how subordinates feel;

- share your expertise with them; they need to learn new information constantly.

Evaluating your boss: good manager, good leader?

You might not realize it, but bosses are expected to

excel in two areas: management and leadership. By learning how to manage your not-so-good boss in these areas, you could turn them into a great boss.

How much you can help your boss depends on how much you're allowed to participate in their decision making and how well you manage them already. Let's look at the ways in which bosses may carry out their management duties. Evaluate where your boss needs help in the following areas:

Managerial role

Strong boss (has it covered)

- Understands his or her role as manager.

- Sees himself or herself as a team leader.

- Accepts managerial responsibility.

- Tries to develop subordinates.

Weaker boss (needs some help)

- Can't distinguish between managerial and non-managerial work.

- Sees himself as The Boss

- Avoids managerial responsibility.

- Is not concerned with employee development.

Duties and job knowledge

Strong boss

- Always open to new things.
- Enjoys and understands job.
- Can handle duties.

Weaker boss

- Has ceased to learn new things.
- Hates job, doesn't understand.
- Job too big.

Communications

Strong boss

- Accessible.
- Initiates.
- Uses a variety of methods.

Weaker boss

- Inaccessible.
- Avoids.
- Uses one method.

How strong a leader is your boss? Does he or she make the whole department feel like a team, inspire others to be like them, or do they seem vaguely embarrassed by a leadership role? Let's look at where your boss could use some help in becoming a more effective leader.

Leadership

Strong boss

- Praises and rewards employees.
- Asks about and monitors employees' progress.
- Helps employees set goals.
- Fosters teamwork.
- Uses conflict constructively.

Weaker boss

- Seldom praises.
- Leaves employees alone.
- Not goal-oriented.
- Treats everyone on a one-to-one basis.
- Avoids conflict at all costs.

Change

Strong boss

- Seeks innovative methods.
- Receptive to new ideas.
- Expects quick change.
- Copes easily with change.

Weaker boss

- Maintains status quo.
- Discourages new ideas.
- Lets things happen slowly.
- Trouble with new procedures.

Decision making

Strong boss

- Flexible.
- Participative.
- Open.
- Enjoys.

Weaker boss

- Rigid.

- Authoritative.

- Closed.

- Avoids.

To help manage your boss, ask yourself some of the following questions:

1. How can I convince my boss to include subordinates in decision making?

2. How can I help my boss overcome his or her fear of confronting employees – particularly when they're angry? My boss's avoidance only heightens emotional conflict.

3. How can I increase the frequency and quality of feedback my boss receives?

4. Can I help my boss be a better team leader by becoming a better team player?

5. What kind of support can I give my boss that will increase his or her visibility within this company?

The answers should help you develop strategies that will improve your boss's management and leadership abilities.

Almost every successful person in business today attributes their style to a good boss who left an impression on them at some point in their career. The successful boss and the subordinate on his or her way up often become fast friends because they instantly recognize similar qualities in each other – leadership qualities they both value.

Learn to value a good boss. And if your boss needs some help before they're *really* good, learn to manage them and you'll have a great relationship.

Summary

In this chapter we've talked about good bosses, who they are, what they can do for you, and how you can manage them.

You can manage a good boss by:

- performing your job well;
- being a good team player;
- showing your boss that you regard him or her as a role model;
- giving them feedback;
- sharing your expertise with them.

Even not-so-good bosses can become good bosses with the help of supportive employees. You can increase your boss's leadership and management skills by:

- evaluating how well they know their job;
- helping them be more flexible;
- keeping them informed;
- supporting their decisions;
- building their visibility within the company.

10

Ten ways to manage your boss

The importance of learning how to manage your boss can't be overemphasized. In today's busy corporate world, subordinates are becoming increasingly more responsible for maintaining a good working relationship with their boss. Ultimately, how well you manage your boss will have more direct bearing on your promotability, your current working conditions and your future career moves than your education and expertise.

Here are the ten commandments for effective boss management:

1.   Have a good grasp of your own strengths

and weaknesses as well as your boss's strengths and weaknesses. You'll know where you two complement each other, where you conflict, where you need help.

2. Know what your boss needs – both work needs and emotional needs. When they're legitimate needs such as loyalty, feedback and support, provide them without having to be coached. Never criticize your boss in front of others. Never underestimate him or her.

3. Understand the rules of team play. Be willing to be a good team player. Your individual contribution has value, but it's greatly enhanced as a part of the group effort. Help your boss become a good team leader.

4. Learn how to build trust. Show your boss you're trustworthy. Demonstrate your trust in them and they'll come through for you. Let your boss know when he or she has violated your trust, has gone beyond the call of duty.

5. Keep the lines of communication open. Give your boss feedback on their performance. Ask questions, rely on his or her guidance. Don't take criticism personally.

6. Share your expertise, innovation and creativity with your boss. Your boss can

learn from you, too, and relies upon you as a problem solver and a source of ideas and skills.

7. Take the initiative, look for solutions to problems and avoid complaining.

8. When problems arise, be straightforward in dealing with them. Develop the confidence and skills to discuss problems with your boss and, if necessary, how you expect your boss's behaviour to change. Always stay objective, concise, professional and calm.

9. If your boss is trying to help you, use him or her as a mentor or networking source. Even good bosses need managing in spots where they're weak. Find out where your boss needs help. Reward your boss's investment in you by performing well. Volunteer for extra projects.

10. Show your boss you understand the duties of management and leadership by incorporating as much of these qualities as you can into your present role. Support your boss's role as manager and leader.

Index

Assertiveness For Managers

Terry Gillen

Flatter organizations, decentralized authority, changing technology, obsolete skills, downsizing, retraining, outplacement - these are common features of today's business environment. Against such a background, success depends increasingly on the personal credibility of individual managers. In this timely book, Terry Gillen explains how an assertive style of management can dramatically improve effectiveness. He sets out the principles and benefits of assertive behaviour and shows how to apply assertiveness techniques in everyday management situations.

Part One places assertiveness in the context of the modern manager's job, illustrates the three main types of behaviour and describes a method of harnessing emotional energy to ensure the desired results. Part Two shows how to handle a range of management problems, including aggressive bosses or colleagues, receiving/giving criticism, disciplining staff, resolving conflict and controlling stress. Each chapter contains examples of the particular problem, guidance on how to deal with it assertively and a summary for rapid reference.

Gower

50 Essential Management Techniques

Michael Ward

Are you familiar with the concept of product life cycle? Of course you are!
Does the prospect of a SWOT analysis bring you out in a cold sweat?
Probably not. But what about the Johari Window? Or Zipf's Law?

Michael Ward's book brings together a formidable array of tools designed to
improve managerial performance. For each entry he introduces the
technique in question, explains how it works, then goes on to show, with
the aid of an entertaining case study, how it can be used to solve an
actual problem. The 50 techniques, including some never before
published, are grouped into eleven subject areas, ranging from strategy to
learning.

For managers in every type of organization and at any level, as well as for
students and consultants, *50 Essential Management Techniques* is likely
to become an indispensable source.

Gower